"Silenced No More"

"*Silenced No More*"

The Courage of a Soldier—
Life After Military Sexual Trauma

Stormie Dunn

authorHOUSE®

AuthorHouse™ LLC
1663 Liberty Drive
Bloomington, IN 47403
www.authorhouse.com
Phone: 1-800-839-8640

Published by AuthorHouse 12/16/2013

ISBN: 978-1-4918-3510-4 (sc)
ISBN: 978-1-4918-3509-8 (hc)
ISBN: 978-1-4918-3508-1 (e)

Library of Congress Control Number: 2013920712

*We were willing
to give our lives
for our country.
In return, our country
has taken our sanity.
However,
we will be
silenced no more!*

Dedication

To all who have suffered from military sexual trauma (MST), those who have survived it, those who have lost their lives because of it, and the families left behind to grieve for those who were victims of it.

To my husband and confidant. Without your love and encouragement, I would not have been able to share my story with you.

To my children. You are my world. You have lived through this hell along with me, and you have suffered at the hands of post-traumatic stress disorder (PTSD) as if it was your burden to carry as well.

To retired U.S. Army Major Timothy Young. You a very special friend who encouraged me to seek God for healing, to speak out until heard and seek justice until satisfied.

To Special Agent Shawn Keyes. Without your dedication and tenacity I would not have found the justice you made possible.

My prayer is for healing of all who have been affected by the nightmare of military sexual trauma. I pray that along with the healing, all families—as well as my children and I—may finally build the strong, healthy relationships we have each needed and form the bonds of a loving family as God intended.

I Wore the Uniform with Pride

I walked the walk with my head held high.

Although I never fought in a war on foreign soil,

I fight a battle full of toil.

Raped by those who were supposed to have your back,

Wanting to hide in the cracks.

Struggling to find a reason,

Why did they commit such treason?

Killing my soul and hope,

Forever sliding further down the slope.

Chasing the demons that consume my nights

Always ready to take flight.

How do I find that which eludes me

When all I can do is flee?

My scars did not come from IEDs or bombs,

They came from a soldier defiling me.

When we were asked what we wanted to be or do when we grew up, none of us woke up and said, "Today, I have made the decision to be raped and have my dignity, self-worth, and pride ripped away. Tomorrow I will live in a constant, crippling fear and avoid sleep due to nightmares."

Oh wait. They chase me even when I am awake. Post-traumatic stress disorder made me spiral out of control. I lost relationships, friendships, jobs, and my family due to the never-ending reaches of depression. I never wanted to drink or use drugs to numb the pain that would never go away. I never wanted to lose the place I once called home and roam the streets on my own. I never wanted the future to include pulling a trigger with shaking hands, swallowing pills, drinking and driving, or committing "suicide by cop" to end the hell I've called life.

How Serious Is the Issue of Military Rape?

Reports of sexual assault in the United States military have inundated local and national media. Due to the extent of coverage across all military branches, it has resulted in a series of scandals and embarrassments that have brought to light a very old problem known as the military's "dirty little secret."

According to the Pentagon, sexual assaults in the military have increased to the alarming level of seventy per day, or three per hour. Twenty-six thousand service members were sexually assaulted in 2012, a 35 percent increase since 2010 when nineteen thousand such cases were reported. However, the overall rate of sexual assault in the US military may be higher because many victims fail to report out of fear of vengeance or lack of justice under the military's system of reporting and prosecution.

Several organizations are currently visiting and calling to compel Senators and their staff to support Sen. Gillibrand's legislation to fundamentally reform the military justice system by passing the MJIA, or Military Justice Improvement Act. The MJIA would take major crimes, including rape and sexual assault outside the chain of command; Americans now recognize that "decisions on whether to prosecute allegations of sexual assault within the military should be made by independent group of military prosecutors instead of within the military chain of command." Our opponents and the Pentagon would like to delay, but Sen. Gillibrand has pledged that come hell or high water we will have our day on the floor of the U.S. Senate this year. She is determined to press for a vote, so all of America can see who truly stands with the men and women in the military, their families, veterans and on the side of fair, impartial justice.

We will redouble our efforts in the coming days to convince all undecided Senators that this vote is foundational to our democracy. Simply put, it is a matter of human rights. Service members deserve a professional, unbiased justice system equal the system afforded to the civilians they protect. You can be part of this reform—Call, Write or email your Senators and demand they support the Military Justice Improvement Act.

As you read this book, both men and women in our military are being sexually harassed and/or sexually assaulted. Gender does not seem to play a role in reported perpetrators; both men and women have committed these atrocities. Precise data for how common sexual assault and harassment are is difficult to give because both crimes often go unreported. History has proven that women are more often sexually victimized than men are; however, men in the military are raped and/or sexually assaulted at an alarming rate as well. Statistics indicate that 23-28 percent of women have reported a sexual assault, but only 3.5 percent of men have reported a sexual assault. However, because men outnumber women in the military, the data indicates that as many men as women have experienced sexual assault.

Another population of the problem that has continued to be overlooked is the children! Below are three cases from June and July 2013. It took approximately thirty seconds to find the three stories on the Internet.

In July 2013, a recently deployed National Guard member was accused of sexually abusing three of his children. The man was indicted on seventeen counts of having sexually abused two twelve-year-olds and one five-year-old according to the chief police officer for the police department. He was the stepfather of one of the children and had adopted the other two. The alleged abuse took place between 2006 and 2012, according to court documents. In addition to sexual battery, the guardsman was also indicted on charges of rape, sexual imposition, and "intimidation of an attorney, victim, or witness in a criminal case."

In June 2013, an air force lieutenant colonel was charged with assaulting and sexually molesting a young girl on multiple occasions between 2005 and 2011, according to a copy of the charge sheet. The alleged incidents occurred in Virginia and Ohio while the lieutenant colonel was assigned to the Pentagon—which is located in Washington, DC. In dozens of incidents detailed on the charge sheet, the air force charged that he engaged in sexual contact with a girl who was younger than twelve years old when the alleged abuse began.

In June 2013, police arrested a twenty-eight-year-old army staff sergeant for sexually assaulting his two juvenile stepdaughters. Police stated that the army staff sergeant was arrested and charged with two counts of continual sexual abuse of a child after police received a report that the stepfather was molesting the two young girls. During the investigation, police determined that the army staff sergeant had sexually assaulted the girls multiple times over the course of five years. Many of the incidents occurred in Arizona, but some may have happened on other military bases around the country.

Once again, I ask, how serious is the issue of military rape? Is this a problem that society should be concerned about? Write down your answers to these questions and review them once you have completed this book to see if your views have changed.

My world twist and spins in this darkness called PTSD

I search for the array of beauty that comes from a rainbow

I try to grasp the golden rays of light given by the sun

I reach for the hope given from prayers

I long to see the world through those rose colored glasses

I strive to see the beauty of a newborn child

I long to feel the love and laughter so many others take for granted

My rainbow is locked inside a twister that never ends

My sun is shrouded in darkness full of anguish

My prayers are locked inside a head full of doubt

My colored glasses are forever coated in black

A newborn child is pitied for the world it will live in

My ears and heart are dead to love and laughter

My world twist and spins in this darkness called PTSD

Army Rank Structure

Rank   **(Non-Commissioned Officers)**

Special   **Sergeant Major of the Army**

There is only one sergeant major of the army. This rank is the epitome of what it means to be a sergeant. This position oversees all non-commissioned officers and serves as the senior enlisted advisor and consultant to the chief of staff of the army, a four-star general.

E-9   **Command Sergeant Major**

Command sergeant majors are the senior enlisted advisors to the commanding officer. They carry out policies and standards, and they advise the commander on the performance, training, appearance, and conduct of enlisted soldiers.

E-9   **Sergeant Major**

Sergeant majors serve as the chief administrative assistants for a headquarters unit of the army, but the sphere of influence regarding leadership is generally limited to those directly under his or her charge. They are key enlisted members of staff at levels of battalion or higher.

E-8   **First Sergeant**

First sergeants are the principal non-commissioned officers and the lifeblood of any company. The provider, disciplinarian, and wise counselor instructs other sergeants, advises the commander, and helps train all enlisted soldiers. They also assist officers at the company level, overseeing from sixty-two up to one hundred and ninety-four soldiers.

E-8   **Master Sergeant**

The principal non-commissioned officer is assigned at the battalion level or higher. They are not charged with all the leadership responsibilities of a first sergeant, but they are expected to dispatch leadership and other duties with the same professionalism.

E-7   **Sergeant First Class**

The assistant and advisor to the platoon leader generally has fifteen to eighteen years of army experience and puts it to use by making quick, accurate decisions in the best interests of the soldiers and the country.

E-6   **Staff Sergeant**

Staff sergeants command a squad of nine to ten soldiers and often have one or more sergeants under their leadership. They are responsible for developing, maintaining, and utilizing the full range of the soldiers' potential.

E-5   **Sergeant**

A sergeant typically commands a squad of nine to ten soldiers. This position is considered to have the greatest impact on soldiers because sergeants oversee them in their daily tasks. In short, sergeants set an example and are the standard for privates to look up to and live up to.

E-4   **Corporal**

As the base of the non-commissioned officer ranks, corporals serve as team leaders of the smallest army units. Like sergeants, they are responsible for individual training, personal appearance, and cleanliness of soldiers.

Rank	(Enlisted Personnel)

E-4   Specialist

This position manages other enlisted soldiers of lower ranks. They must have served a minimum of two years and attended a specific training class in order to earn this promotion. People enlisting with a four-year college degree can enter basic combat training as a specialist.

E-3   Private First Class

Private (PV2s) may be promoted to this level after one year (or earlier at the request of supervisor). Individuals can begin basic combat training at this level with experience or prior military training. PV2s carry out orders issued to them to the best of their abilities.

E-2   Private

Private is the lowest rank. This position is a trainee who is starting basic combat training. The primary role of this position is to carry out orders to the best of his or her ability.

E-1   Private (Recruit)

Private recruits do not have an insignia.

"I, Stormie Dunn, do solemnly swear (or affirm) that I will
support and defend the Constitution of the United States
against all enemies, foreign and domestic; that I will bear
true faith and allegiance to the same; and that I will obey the
orders of the president of the United States and the orders of
the officers appointed over me, according to regulations and
the Uniform Code of Military Justice. So help me God."

During the fall of 1961 in Houston, Texas, a beautiful and bewitching young woman and a devilishly charismatic young man met by chance and fell in love in a whirlwind romance. For Victoria, it was love at first sight, and the magic of that love discovered so long ago still brings a wishful smile as she speaks about the mesmerizing man who stole her heart while sweeping her off her feet.

She was entranced by the insolent and debonair man who made her heart race and her stomach flutter with just a glance. He was different from the farm boys she had dated. He had an air of surliness about him, faced the world with a try, and a stop-me-if-you-dare attitude. Victoria, as a quiet and reserved person, found him to be fascinating, and she could not understand what he saw in her—she was just a girl from the farm.

William was going steady with his sister Paula's best friend, Connie, when he found himself spellbound by Victoria's beauty and innocence. Although they had only been going steady for six months, Connie had the notions of marrying William someday and believing in her dreams. She even bought a wedding dress for when they eloped. Connie had accepted that she could never have a church wedding to William since her parents detested the arrogant young man.

William's sisters were excited to hear he had met another young woman who was able to enchant him enough that he intended to propose. Even though his sisters liked Connie, they could not imagine them married and were happy for him. Connie was a docile Suzy Homemaker, and William would have broken her spirit without much effort. Victoria, however, grew up with a passel of brothers and could stop any of them with just a look; she was just the match William needed to tame his wild streak.

In no time at all, William had proposed to Victoria, and he was elated when she accepted. He was eager to plan a wedding, and William's sisters wanted to know if a date had been set. Bashfully, Victoria replied she would have to save for a dress before she would set a date. As the four women sat around talking, Paula, the oldest of William's three sisters, suddenly drew in a deep breath that startled the other women. Concerned about her, they asked if she was all right.

Jumping up, Paula said, "Fine—but I need to go. I will be back soon."

An idea had suddenly come to Paula; she knew she could get a beautiful dress from her best friend. She called Connie and explained that she needed a nice dress because she had met a special young man and wanted to elope with him. As the girls talked and Connie was asking Paula about her young man, she thought that Paula could use her dress. She offered to loan Paula her most prized dress, the one she would wear to wed William someday. Little did she know the dress made its debut at William's wedding. However, on that magical day, she was not the one wearing it.

On January 6, 1962, William and Victoria vowed to love, honor, and cherish each other until death do them part. They began a new journey as man and wife. Marrying at the young age of eighteen is frowned upon within today's society; however, it was the norm for their time. William had turned nineteen two days prior, and Victoria was three months shy of her eighteenth birthday. They had the world to conquer when they wed. They looked forward to a future filled with love, romance, and adventure—along with the thrill of being out from under their parents' roofs. It was their time now!

Up to that point in his life, William had held no fantasies about life. He knew all too well how hard and cruel life could be, even to a child. His father raised William and his seven siblings in a single-parent household. Their mother had walked out on them when they were young and still in need of a mother's love, tender words, and caresses. She abandoned her family to follow another man to California where she married and started a new family without looking back. Try as he may, William's father could not support them on just his earnings; therefore, William and several of his brothers had to drop out of school to help support the younger siblings. Any protest led to the father's pounding fist or a whip to the backside. He was a cruel, heavy-handed man who did not need a reason to raise his hand to them.

Victoria, however, came from a dual-parent household along with eight younger siblings. Although her mother did not work outside of the home, Victoria, just a child herself, had to help look after her younger siblings. With nine children underfoot, there were more chores than just one person could manage. By five years old, Victoria was cooking, cleaning, doing laundry, and caring for the babies. Several of her siblings believed she was the mother because she was the one they remember cooking, feeding, and caring for them. They turned to her for comfort if hurt, scared, or just needed attention.

Victoria often woke to find one or more siblings curled up on the twin bed with her. When they were older, the roles reversed; the boys chaperoned Victoria on dates to protect her integrity and reputation as customs of the time dictated. Spare moments were few and far in between for Victoria, but when she was rewarded with them, she filled them with dreams of traveling. She longed to finish high school and nursing school and then travel around the world to the magical destinations she had discovered while reading.

Having earned a Silver Star during World War II in the army, Victoria's father was honorably discharged; however, with nine mouths to feed, he needed a job. Soon, Hank was putting some of the skills learned during his enlistment to good use. He began driving eighteen-wheelers for a living, and after putting in a day's hard work, he liked to visit the local bars and throw back a couple of ice-cold beers and shoot a game or two of pool.

On one such occasion, as was Hank's habit with a few too many libations, his alligator mouth overran his mosquito ass. He proceeded to run his mouth to some of the other patrons about a job that his company had won a bid. Apparently, he was boasting to a pit of angry rattlesnakes because several of the men had lost their jobs due to Hank's underbidding a job their company had bid on as well. As he continued to gloat about his success, the men became angry. An argument quickly ensued. The bartender, not about to have his bar torn apart, threw them all out in hopes of ending the confrontation before someone ended up hurt or dead. Unfortunately, it was not to be. What happened next is only speculation since Hank seldom spoke of the incident.

A couple of nights after the altercation at the bar, a monumental snowstorm dropped layers of thick, freezing snow. Knowing his wife would be worried, Hank called from the bar to say he was on his way home, hoping to keep her and the kids from worrying about him. He assured her that he would leave as soon as they ended their call, promising to be home for dinnertime. Still worried about the escalating snowstorm, Alice cautioned him with weather warnings, which were predicting a closure of the mountain pass. Alice urged Hank to be safe and hurry home before the storm trapped him on the other side of the mountain. For once, he did just as he had promised and headed for home.

The fieriness of the storm had Alice alternating between nervous pacing and anxiously praying as she waited for Hank's arrival; however, he never made it home. After several hours, Alice decided to call the police, which upon hearing her concerns, recommended she call the state police. After recalling her conversation with Hank along with his assurance of leaving for home in hopes of beating the storm however had failed to show, she asked the state police for help. Pleading with them to search for Hank and explaining he was driving a blue eighteen-wheeler with an American flag painted on the doors, Alice recited the route Hank routinely traveled from the bar through

17

the mountain pass. They attempted to assure her that Hank was more than likely safe and would probably be home any minute now; however, they agreed to look for him, weather permitting.

Units assigned to patrolling that section of the road began searching for a blue eighteen-wheeler matching the information Alice had provided. The search began from the bar Hank had phoned from and ended at the mountain pass. The truck was located, still running, parked in middle of the road, just before the mountain pass. A downed tree was blocking the road. The state police found Hank unconscious not far from the cab of his truck; he had been beaten half to death. They also discovered a bloody tire iron a short distance away and came to a preliminary consensus; they believed it to be the weapon used in the assault.

The police called Alice to inform her that Hank had been located. Since he was injured and en route to the local hospital, they suggested getting to the hospital as quickly as possible without putting herself in danger on the frozen roadways. She pled with the officer to tell her what had happened to Hank. The officer explained that Hank was a lucky man to have survived the beating, but surviving in the frozen, snow-covered road for several hours was a miracle.

It took a couple of months of healing—along with grueling sessions of physical therapy—before Hank accepted being a quadriplegic. At times, he could not wrap his mind around the fact that he would never have use of his body from the waist down again. Alice was ecstatic to hear Hank would survive, and the reality that he was a paraplegic and would never walk again did not register in her mind. At that moment, all she heard was the father of her children, her lover, had survived and would be coming home soon. Alice prayed for his recovery so often that her knees where raw from kneeling. As terrifying as Hank's stay in the hospital was for the family, Alice was more terrified of what life would have been like had he not survived.

As Hank progressed in his recovery, Alice understood that he had lost the use of his body from the waist down forever. She was thankful that he survived and looked forward having him at home again. Life without him had been lonely, and the hours seemed to stretch on forever.

After many arduous months of physical therapy, Hank was finally coming home. On the day of his release, Alice made a vow that she would love, stand by, and care for him until their dying days. During Hank's hospitalization, their sons and son-in-laws had built a ramp to give him easy access to the house. They added handrails since the physical therapist believed that with encouragement and work, he would be able to walk with leg braces and crutches. A van was adapted with special equipment that allowed him to work the gas and brakes with hand levers. He adapted to his new life with some bumps here and there. Driving helped him maintain some dignity and purpose.

However, as the years passed, Hank became bitter at being crippled. He gave up trying to do anything for himself, and Alice became resentful at being left to constantly care for and live with a crippled man who no longer cared.

Hank refused to do many of the things could still do for himself, such as making coffee or fixing something to eat. There was nothing wrong from the waist up; his arms and hands functioned as well as anyone else's did. The years passed slowly, and the pressures of having to care for Hank began to affect Alice mentally and physically. The constant demands on her shoulders became more than she could bear. Alice, already a petite woman, paid a dear price for her care. It definitely took its toll on her body; she passed away in her early sixties, long before her time. He lived another eight years in misery and regret.

Hank and Alice did not care one bit for William, seeing through his facade that had fooled so many others. Truth be told, none of her siblings cared much for him either. When he came to ask for Victoria's hand in marriage, Alice would not give her permission until Victoria had graduated from nursing school. Many said that Alice had the foresight to know Victoria would need her nursing skills to survive. That one demand turned out to be a blessing in disguise.

Neither William nor Victoria had much of an opportunity to be a child or to experience the freedom of being a carefree teenager due to having to step into the roles of adults from a very early age. Therefore, they did not mentally or physically cultivate the many milestones young children experience and learn from as they grow and mature.

It has been debated whether William and Victoria became dysfunctional adults and parents due to the loss of their childhood and skills that are cultivated during childhood; essentially, they never developed who they were as people. Many believe that William and Victoria rushed into marriage as a way to get out of their parents' homes, which afforded them the opportunity to live their own lives. That was something they had never done.

They had hopes and dreams for living on their own, of being carefree and free of responsibility for the first time in their lives. However, the freedom they so craved and the carefree life they had envisioned and dreamt about did not last long. Two months after the wedding, Victoria was shocked when she discovered she was pregnant. To say that William was not happy would be putting it mildly.

In November 1962, Victoria gave birth her first bubbly, healthy boy, Chad. Bryan, another bubbly, healthy boy, was born in 1964. Two years later, Stormie, a beautiful healthy baby girl was born. Just eleven short months later, Carlee, another beautiful healthy baby girl, was born. They were once again raising children.

When we were young, we loved listening to our mom tell us stories from her days as a nurse. She has always said that she loved working as a pediatric nurse the most, but working in the neonatal care unit was her favorite. Her voice would fill with such pride as she told us about working with newborn babies. Mom often said there was nothing more rewarding than seeing a tiny struggling infant grow and become healthy enough to go home. She said it was like seeing a miracle from God. My mother has never forgotten those days, and it is sad to hear her say that it was only during her days of nursing that she ever felt a sense of pride in herself. Her skills as a nurse kept us fed as small children, and it broke her heart when, due to financial hardships, she was not able to keep her nursing licenses. She still feels that loss and regret today.

Over the years, our parents had several jobs, including owning two different restaurants. We all worked endless hours, struggling to make them successful. I remember being seven or eight years old having to wash dishes, clear tables, and help keep the customers drinks filled with my siblings. After the restaurant closed for the evening, it was our job to clean the tables, refill the salt and peppershakers, sweep, and mop the floors. It was only after finishing chores at the restaurant that we could go home to complete our chores and homework before bedtime.

On weekends, when other kids were watching cartoons or playing outside, we were working in the restaurant or cooking and cleaning at home. It was not bad all the time; Mom did not open the restaurant when my father was gone with his latest tryst, which allowed us to forgo our chores, play outside, or watch television. There were other fun occasions, especially when family or friends of our parents came to visit and brought their children. More often than not, most of our childhood days were spent on chores instead of playing. Laughter was not a complete stranger to us; there were some good memories, just not enough.

Eventually, like so many other small mom-and-pop establishments, our parents called it quits. They closed both of the restaurants after a year or so due to financial losses and my father's never-ending flings with the servers. Mom once admitted that she used us to perform the servers' tasks because she could not trust my father with them, and she refused to hire another one. Mom did not have many friends and certainly not any close female friends because of my father's roaming eyes and hands. We do not recall ever seeing her have a girl's night out or a girl's *anything*. The only people she seemed comfortable around were her co-workers at the police department. Mom's life was spent going to work and then home to sleep to wake up and do it again. There was no dining out, movies, or anything other than the occasional school event.

Shortly after selling the last restaurant, my mother became a dispatcher for the local police department. Mom always worked long hours—usually at minimal pay—to support us. She never wavered from that, until late 2001, when my father was diagnosed with terminal lung cancer and required home care. Mom resigned once dad required full-time care through his last days. He passed away in April 2002.

Mom returned to work after his death due to financial needs; however, she just could not keep up the hectic pace required as a dispatcher. Caring for him wore heavily on a body already deteriorated from years of uncontrollable blood sugar spikes, obesity, and chronic depression. Due to the overwhelming burdens life placed on her, her health has suffered greatly. Her eyesight is almost gone as the blood sugar spikes wreaked havoc on her body, including the small capillaries behind the eyes. The pressure caused them to rupture, and although designed to repair themselves, scar tissue built up and began to affect her eyesight.

She suffered two strokes and three mini-strokes in the past year, causing weakness to the right side of her body, stuttering, loss of balance, and memory loss. Due to the loss of balance, Mom has fallen six or seven times in the last six months, and each time, it has taken her longer to recover. Chad has moved in to care for her, and we could not be more grateful; without him, Mom would be in a home. We fear that she has just given up on life and is just waiting to join her loved ones in heaven. We have talked to her about this and have even tried to get her to visit the community center where she could meet some people her own age, but she is like a kindergartener on the first day of school. When we take her there, she stays for an hour and then has them call us to pick her up. When asked why she did not stay longer, she uses her sight as an excuse. She says she cannot see the cards or puzzle pieces; however, when we tell her she could always just sit and talk and get to know people her own age, she gets pouty.

During my father's life, he held numerous jobs, and it is impossible to remember them all. He was a welder, a roadside tire repair technician, jailer, deputy, restaurant owner, and a machine shop owner. He was a jack-of-all-trades and could fix toasters, air conditioners, lawnmowers, and automobiles. He was famous for buying things cheap and repairing, repainting, and selling them for three times what he had paid for them. His talent supplemented Mom's income when he chose to contribute. However, because of his hot temper and short fuse, he never kept a job for too long. He worked where he wanted when he wanted. More often than not, it was my mother's responsibility to pay the bills and see to it that we had food to eat and clothes to wear.

After having to help raise his siblings, my father had no desire to have kids of his own, and he made sure we knew that every single day. Whenever my mother was at work or sleeping, we often found ourselves left in our father's care—if he stayed around long enough for us to be. As children, we were always having "accidents" that left us bruised and battered. We learned to lie about what had caused the bruises at a very early age because telling the truth only earned us more. On one occasion while he was supposed to watch us, a portable heater fell into the crib while I was napping, landing on my right thigh.

I had second—and third-degree burns. To this day, the scar is still visible.

One year, a neighbor gave us a swing set. When my father assembled it, he ran out of hardware and did not bolt the slide onto the swing set. Being a child and not knowing any better, while sliding, the slide flipped over and the metal on the underside ripped open my shin, requiring forty-seven stitches.

When I was five, while drawing water from the well, he leaned over to pull the bucket out and a package of his cigarettes fell out of his shirt pocket and into the well. After several failed attempts at lowering the bucket into the water and trying to scoop up the cigarettes, he called the girls over to the well. He told us that he was going to hold one of us by our ankles and lower us into the well to get his cigarettes.

Carlee was the quickest to react and said she was not doing it and ran into the house. Left standing there with no other choice, I was lifted by the waist and sat on the side of the well. Taking hold of my ankles, he lowered me into the well until I was able to retrieve his cigarettes. His only thought was for those cigarettes; it never occurred to him how much danger I had been placed in.

At seven years old, our cat tore a window screen in our brother's room. When my father saw the rip, he became uncontrollably enraged. He started screaming, cussing, and demanding to know which one of us "lazy, no good for nothing piece of shits" had torn the window screen. When we told him it was Blackie, he did not believe us—or he believed and just did not care because he'd had a bad day or someone had pissed him off. As was often his habit, he took it out on us. He lined us up from oldest to youngest; he gave us five pops and then sent us to get back in line for another round. He would do this repeatedly until one of us said we had done it. On this occasion, Chad took the blame in an effort to prevent us from being beaten any more than we had already endured. My father beat him so badly that he missed two weeks of school. My mother kept him home, fearing someone would see the bruises and report it.

When I was ten, a neighbor's home was broken into. When my father came in from working, the homeowner came over and accused Bryan and his friends. No sooner had the door shut than my father snatched Bryan up by his hair and started beating him with a belt. When the belt broke, he started using his fist. We could hear Bryan begging him to stop while trying to tell him that he had not done it. My mother tried to intercede, begging my father to stop, but he just kept on beating him. After what seemed like hours, she managed to get between them. When she threatened to call the police, he finally stopped.

To this day, we do not know why he stopped beating Bryan. He knew that Mom would not call the police because she never did. It often seemed like my father hated Bryan, and as we got older, he took the brunt of my father's anger and abuse. He has since separated himself from our family and currently lives with his family in another state.

At thirteen, my father gave me one of the worst beatings of my life. When we arrived home from school, there was always a chore list waiting. We knew the chores had to be completed to my father's standards by the time he came home from work. On that particular day, mowing the lawn was my assigned chore. Our father's rule was that once you completed mowing the yard, you were to rake and bag the clippings, wash the mower down before putting it away, and then roll the water hose back up. After mowing the lawn, raking, and bagging the clippings, washing and putting away the mower, a shower was in order. After all that work, feeling hot and dirty, a shower was just what I needed..

The cold water felt so good after being out in the heat for so long. However, it did not last very long. My father arrived home from work, and as he pulled up to the house, he noticed the hose I had forgotten to roll up. Before I knew what was happening, he grabbed a handful of hair and jerked me out of the shower with barely enough time to grab a towel to cover myself. As he dragged me outside, he screamed and cussed at me. He screamed, "How many times do you have to be told to do something before it sinks into your thick head."

He reached down, picked up a rope, and started hitting me with it. He didn't care where it landed. He used that rope until I had the water hose rolled back up—his way. By the time he finished, I had welts from head to toe. I often wanted to ask him if he still felt that a water hose was worth that beating—or if any of the beating were worth the supposed wrongdoings.

Carlee was not exempt from his beatings either. At meals, she was terrified pick up to her drink because she knew if she spilt any of it, he would spank her and then make her lick it up. It did not matter to him if she was licking it from the table or the floor. Because of bed-wetting, Carlee could not have anything to drink after five o'clock, which we believed was caused by fear of my father. When she was just four or five, if she wet the bed, he would spank her, make her strip the bed, and tell her to wash and dry the sheets before remaking the bed. It did not matter what time it was or whether we had school the next day. In middle of the night, she would often crawl into bed and curl up next to me as if I were her safety blanket.

We believed that my mother looked the other way because she did not know how to be on her own and was afraid of taking care of four children by herself. Mom never understood that she had already been doing that our entire lives. Mom kept our family together with promises that things would get better, but they never did.

As adults, we learned that my mother had attempted to leave several times; however, none in her family was willing to take us into their homes. The boys slept in bunk beds and when our father saw a tear in the box spring lining of the upper bed, he beat them. That beating gave her the courage to ask her parents to take us in.

Our grandmother said, "You made your bed, now sleep in it." However, the kids suffered the most. For as often as he beat us, he never lifted a hand to my mother.

When we were small kids, during one of the coldest Oklahoma winters, our parents were evicted. We had to move to a great-aunt's garage. With six people cramped into such a small space, we hung sheets across a wire to divide the room into living spaces and bedrooms. Our beds were twin mattresses on the floor; the girls shared one, and the boys shared another. There was no bathroom in the garage; we either hiked out to the outhouse or used a five-gallon bucket as a makeshift toilet. Whoever was unlucky enough to cause it to reach the halfway point had to carry it out to the pasture to dispose of the waste, wash the bucket out, and return it to its rightful place.

It snowed so badly that winter that the snow was higher than the doorframe. We were snowbound for almost a week; a potbelly stove kept us warm and fed during those long days. My father was meaner than a bear after a couple of days, and we knew to stay out of his way. We did not make too much noise when playing; in fact, we stayed in our makeshift rooms a majority of the time just to avoid him.

I once backed toward that old stove for warmth, and it left a mark that is still visible on my left thigh. On another occasion, my long auburn hair was singed so much that it had to be cut almost as short as my brother's hair. As much as we loved the warmth from that stove—and the many meals prepared on it—we also hated it because it was our job to trek out to the woodpile to gather the wood and carry it into the house so it could dry out before burning it. It did not matter if it was snowing, raining, or sunshine. The wood was essential for our heating and cooking needs, and it was our job to bring it in.

Lugging the firewood was just one of the many chores we learned as young children. While most other kids were sleeping, we were being woken up two hours earlier than needed before school in order to work in the garden, gather eggs, and feed and milk our dairy cow. Only after all the chores were finished to my father's satisfaction would he allow us to go inside to clean up for breakfast—if we had time to eat—and get dressed for school.

During the summer, we ran around barefoot unless it was Sunday. On Sundays, we wore our best clothes and shoes because the rest of the family would be there. Dad's pride often saw us go without rather than accepting help. When I joined the Brownies, my parents could not afford the uniform. When the Brownie leader, our principal's wife, came by to give me a uniform she had bought, my father threw it back at her and said, "We do not take charity." He slammed the door in her face; needless to say, I never attended another meeting.

For the first part of our lives, when the doors to the church were open, we were there. We still do not know if our parents actually believed or if they were there because the rest of our family attended.

We were raised Pentecostal, which meant the girls were not allowed to wear pants. Carlee and I—and all our female cousins—wore old tattered coats and dresses while walking half a mile to and from the bus stop during the freezing rain and snow.

Those memories are why I still dislike the cold and snow; however, as a child, some of my fondest winter memories are of making peanut brittle with our grandmother, snow angels, and snowball fights.

We filled the summers with adventures. We explored in the woods, roasted marshmallows over the brick oven in our grandparents' back yard, caught fireflies, and climbed the cherry tree and ate until we were caught or full. It was our favorite time of year because we left after breakfast and did not return until called in for dinner or dusk began creeping in. We often slept on our grandparents' front porch in sleeping bags and bathed in the creek that ran behind their house. However, one of the fondest memories was when the adults put in a sidewalk. After pouring the cement, the kids placed marbles throughout the length. We had a blast deciding where the marbles would be placed and by whom.

Those early years were the only time we lived close to any of our extended family. On Sundays, we would all gather at Granny's house for supper. Each family would bring a covered dish, and after grace, we would eat like kings. Often we ate more than our share because we knew that we might not have much to eat that coming week. Our dinners mostly consisted of cornbread, fresh cow's milk, beans, and rice or fried potatoes. Leftover rice became breakfast by adding a dab of butter and a teaspoon of sugar; leftover mashed potatoes became potato cakes. Nothing was ever wasted or taken for granted in our home.

After Sunday supper, the men would head outside to smoke and talk while the boys chased each other around the yard playing tag or Cowboys and Indians. The smaller children napped on makeshift pallets while the women and girls gathered around the dining table to talk and catch up with each other. Once supper was cleared and the dishes were washed, a suspended quilting square was lowered, and the women quilted while they talked. Many of life's lessons were taught and learned as another quilt was pieced together and sewn at Granny's table. We made the quilts with outgrown shirts, old dresses, and worn-out jeans.

Our families began to grow apart—as most families do—and some moved all over the United States. Uncle Gavin married and moved to Texas to attend law school. Uncle Roger joined the army and left to fight in Vietnam. Aunt Julie married and moved away, and soon the rest of my mother's siblings did too. We left Oklahoma and settled in Texas. We would never reclaim that lost family bond or experience the closeness and security that came with being raised by a community or an extended family.

We do not know much about my father's family other than his mother left them when they were young to follow another man to California. We heard that our grandfather was a hard, ruthless man with a heavy hand when it concerned his kids. If true, it would explain a lot about my father since he had a heavy hand when it came to his children.

We would visit a couple of my father's siblings from time to time but never long enough to know any of them that well. Uncle Calvin and Uncle Walter were the only two we even knew well enough to say we knew them, but even that was limited. For most of our lives, it was just our parents and the kids, probably to hide the abuse we endured.

For most of our lives, we raised ourselves because our mom was either at work or sleeping, and my father would often take off with his current girlfriend. After a month-long fling, he would return home as if he had never left. We never understood my mother's weakness when it came to him. Time after time, she would forgive him and let him back into our lives—no matter how may lies he told. He said whatever she wanted to hear; he promised things would be different if she would just give him one more chance. And she always did.

It was easier for her to forgive him than to face being a single parent. In hindsight, she realizes that being a single parent would have been so much better than what we lived through at the hands of my father. To this day, we do not think she realizes that she was a single parent for most of our lives. She was the one who kept us together and made sure we were fed, clothed, and had a home.

My mother became severely depressed after my father left with another woman. His litany of lies and betrayals had left her devastated for the last time. She could not see the point of living without him anymore and attempted suicide by overdosing on her prescription medications. It was only by the grace of God that she survived. One of our neighbors had dropped in for a visit and found her unconscious on the floor. Had it not been for her, my mother would not be with us. It terrified us to imagine life with just my father.

That day, they called us out of class to the counselor's office and informed us that a neighbor was coming to pick us up because my mother was in the hospital. Since my father had just taken off with another woman—and knowing how depressed she had been lately—we knew it was not going to be good news.

I can still see that frightened little girl, terrified of her mother dying and being raised by her father. We never knew when his next beating or cussing would happen or why. Most of the time, there was no reason other than he hated himself and the world and we were handy targets. My father told us almost daily that we were stupid, worthless, and would never amount to anything. He made sure we knew we were never wanted and that he had to sacrifice everything because of us.

From the beginning, I did not belong. I felt like an imposter; it was as if they were not my real parents or my real family. Countless hours of daydreaming about my real parents and what they were like gave me hope. Those parents were going to show up one day to rescue me and take me home where I would be loved and wanted. However, like most dreams, it did not come true. Reading consumed any time not spent daydreaming. Under the porch was the best hideaway; I read by the soft glow of a flashlight, hosting picnics, vacations, and lavish galas. Through reading, I transcended reality in the worlds created by different authors. Reading was a passion; I could be on an African safari or falling in love with a laird in Scotland. I still have a great fondness for reading and fervidly anticipate more journeys with each new book. Reading was the only thing my father could not take away, and he did not exist when I was reading.

My father's lack of work ethic and lousy attitude resulted in us moving seventeen times by the time I was in the eleventh grade. We never stayed in one place long enough to settle in, feel at home, or to make any lasting friendships. However, in June 1978, we finally settled down in a small East Texas town. I was in fifth grade. This was the first and last place we lived long enough to become a part of the school and the community. The constant moving resulted in education problems for all the kids. My nemesis was speech; I had difficulty pronouncing words with a C or an S.

My fifth grade teacher made life hell during the first few months of school. She would call on me to read aloud every single day, or so it seemed, even knowing the shame and embarrassment it would cost. It made me dread going to school. I didn't realize at the time that she was just trying to help. After a couple of months, she requested a referral to the special education reading class; somehow my hatred toward her increased. However, by the end of the year, my speech and reading had improved so much that I competed at State UIL, or

University Interscholastic League. UIL exists to provide educational extracurricular academic, athletic, and music contests. The UIL was created by The University of Texas at Austin in 1910 and has grown into the largest inter-school organization of its kind in the world. I competed in two areas, competition in prose and in poetry. I placed second, and for the first time in my life, I knew what it felt like to be proud of myself. For the past twenty years, I have often thought about going back and telling her how her concern had a profound and lasting effect on me. I never got around to it, and I lost the opportunity to say thank you when she passed away in 2012.

In Chester Texas, we participated in every sport and activity available; there were two reasons behind this. It enabled us to stay away from home as much as possible, and it felt good to feel like a part of something for the first time. Being teased for my thrift store clothing did not help my confidence.

The junior high announced cheerleading tryouts, and I wanted to sign up more than anything. Even though I did not believe I had even a sliver of a chance to be selected, I mustered the courage and signed up. Shaking, I walked to the middle of the gym. I performed my cheer in front of the entire student body. With a racing heart, sweaty palms, and shaking legs, my performance was actually good. When I was selected for the team, I was shocked, amazed, and overwhelmed.

In the marching band, the clarinet players competed for first and second chair in the clarinet section. I was not able to read sheet music because I played by ear, but I memorized the tunes and was selected for second chair. In track, the relay team and forty-yard dash filled my days, and I experienced happiness and belonging for the first time.

We were finally getting to experience being kids and teenagers. We spend nights with friends, rode four-wheelers, went mudding, and stood around an open fire, talking and living life. Each of us found a group that we fit into, and sometimes the groups overlapped. As bad as our lives had been, this newfound happiness kept us going.

In that quaint East Texas town, I experienced the first flutters of love with Dooley. During the summers, the older boys would gather at the baseball field, and that was where he captured my heart. He had the cutest smile that traveled all the way to his eyes. He loved to make people laugh and did so often. Like a silly girl, I dreamed I would be his wife someday. I loved that fearless boy, but it didn't last. However, we had fun. Dooley bought his first new truck while we dated. He was proud of that truck, and I loved the color combination he chose. It was maroon with a silver stripe that ran along its side. I will never forget him teaching me how to drive his truck. He also taught me to jump the old dirt road bridges in his truck; we would go out to the old dirt roads that still have the wood bridges and go really fast so that when you started over the bridge, the buildup of dirt to transcend from road to bridge would propel the truck into the air. We also viewed my first romantic sunset together in that truck. He held a special place in my heart, and he still does. Although we met thirty-one years ago and have lived oceans apart at times, we have kept in contact through the years. He got married, raised seven kids, and owns a cafe in Corrigan, Texas. Although I was heartbroken, Garth Brooks was right when he said, "Thank God for unanswered prayers."

Just like all high schools, ours had little cliques. In that small town, social status was dependent upon your last name, who you were kin to, and who invited you into a group. There were also typical pranks; sometimes we pulled them on others, and at other times, we were the targets. One year, a girl on my basketball team thought she was Miss America. Sarah, Carlee, and I had had enough of her attitude and decided to give her an adjustment. We confiscated some skunk oil spray of our brothers and strategically placed several drops on her gym clothes. There was only one problem with this; we did not think it through. When my class entered the locker room, the smell made our eyes water and made us gag. It took everything to change into our gym clothes. It took a while before she figured the smell was coming from her, but once she did, she was mad as hell.

My father went to the hospital in Houston for open-heart surgery. Since it was two hours from where we lived, Mom stayed in his room with him. Carlee felt guilty and tattled on us. Since my parents were gone, the principal assigned each of us to a week's detention. Sarah was assigned to the history teacher's room, Carlee was assigned to science teacher's room, and the math teacher was blessed with me for a whole week. Sarah and Carlee were pissed because they were assigned to the disciplinarians' classrooms, and I was sitting in the heartthrob teacher's classroom. Most of the girls had a crush on him. The skunk oil had been my idea, and I was the one who visited the locker room that day. Sarah and Carlee were so mad at me; they had conspired with me and received the worse punishment. We thought it was so funny back then, but in hindsight, we regret having been so cruel to someone else. We did not enjoy being teased or embarrassed, and we should never have enjoyed doing it to another human being. If you are reading this book, I am sorry for the hurt and embarrassment we caused you with that cruel prank.

Mrs. Marianne taught us that God had a path planned, even though we could not always see it or understand it. She was a blessing to all the neighborhood kids. If she could share God's word with you, listen to your troubles, or give advice for an asked question, she was always there. She was the first adult to reach out to us kids. She could see that we desperately needed something or someone positive and supporting in our lives. The world would be a better place if it had more people like Mrs. Marianne in it. She held us accountable for our actions but gave us encouragement as well. She showed us how to live a godly life, and that faith she instilled so deeply is still a guide. Saying she is an incredible woman does not do her justice. She is truly one of God's angels sent to walk among us. During a homecoming reunion last year, I was blessed to visit with Mrs. Marianne. I thanked God that she had not changed a bit. Seeing and talking to her was like taking a step back in time.

However, not everyone in that town had a loving generous heart like Mrs. Marianne. My high school English teacher was so hateful; she put down her students and embarrassed us in class because she could. Her meanness was not limited to the students she did not like; it spilled over onto my history teacher. My English teacher would have her "pets" do things to intentionally torture the history teacher.

She played a large part in my brothers dropping out of school. After all, if someone who is supposed to shape your mind says you will never accomplish anything, why would you continue going? I wonder if my brothers were the only ones she made drop out. It makes me shudder to think of the many students she discouraged or who gave up because of her over the years. She let many opportunities slip through her grasp; educators are the ones who shape the minds of tomorrow's leaders. Other than Mrs. Taylor, we had some exceptional teachers who positively affected many students.

We each had a few great friends. Chad had Jackie and Greg. Bryan had Brad and Tony. Carlee had Brianna and Julie. And I had Samantha, Cali, and Fannie. That town was filled with many wonderful people who have stayed with us in our memories.

In 1983, we moved to Groveton, Texas. I started tenth grade in another rural town. My parents managed to keep us there for the entire school year. However, just as we began to settle in and make friends, they informed us that we were moving to Livingston, Texas. Every time we moved, it was to another form of the hick town we had just left behind. Sick of life at home and sick of moving, going with them again was not going to happen. A friend's parents were kind enough to allow me to live with them. I stayed there until halfway through the eleventh grade. Sick of home and school, my brothers had already dropped out of high school and left home.

A few months into the eleventh grade, my mom finally kicked my father out. This time, he was not coming back. She was filing for divorce. She and Carlee wanted me to come home, and against my gut feeling, I did.

Within a few months of being home, my father had once again talked his way back into my house and Mom's heart. Preferring to live with friends even if it meant sleeping on the floor, it did not take very long to pack, leave, and find a full-time job at McDonald's to pay one-third of the rent while going to school. My father believed that all life held for me was to end up barefoot and pregnant, dropping out of school, and never amounting to anything. Not only was there no baby, there was no dropping out of school. After graduating from high school, I accomplished a lot with my life. I guess he did not know everything after all.

The only good thing to come from that last move was meeting a wonderful, captivating, charming young man. Within weeks, Scott and I were going steady; before we realized it, we were head over hills in love. Scott proposed the following summer, and we were married on August 25, 1985, just days before starting my senior year. Many people, including family and friends, assumed pregnancy was the only reason we married so young and so soon. It was hilarious to see them watching and waiting for a baby that was never there. They just could not accept that we married at seventeen because we were in love and did not want to wait to start our lives together. Many people had egg on their faces when there was no baby nine months later. For years, we laughed when we recalled the looks on their faces.

Since we both came from abusive homes, we dreamed of escaping our small town and making something out of our lives. We did not want to be like our parents and live paycheck to paycheck. We did not know how we were going to accomplish it, but we knew we would. The answer to our dreams arrived during a junior-senior class assembly. An army recruiter gave a presentation and detailed all the benefits that came along with being a soldier. By joining, we could earn educational benefits and travel the world. We knew instantly that it was the answer to our prayers. We were so excited when our best friend decided to join as well. Like the Three Musketeers, we were always together. We skipped English class to eat at El Burrito, hung out, watched movies, or listened to country music, and drove around. Bill was part of our family; we loved him like a brother. To this day, we remain friends.

When he got married, Tammy became a part of our family; likewise, she accepted us into her family.

Like so many other poverty-ridden kids, we turned to the military because of the lure of college, travel, and medical benefits. For most of us, it was the first time we had it—and a guaranteed paycheck. Unfortunately, that is still true today among the lower socioeconomic populations. The mass majority of enlisted personnel come from impoverished, abusive, single-parent families, or the foster care system. Those kids are searching for a better life, a way to attend college, or just a way to get the hell out of where we they are. We believed the military was our only hope and an opportunity to build a better future. It was our miracle.

Like many others, we passed the Armed Services Vocational Aptitude Battery and enlisted. At seventeen, we had to enter under the delayed entry program, which meant that we were committed to enlisting upon our graduation and becoming eighteen years of age. Two months after graduation, we left for boot camp.

Scott's basic training was at Fort Hood, Texas, and he excelled as a soldier. He was the platoon sergeant and was at the top of his class. There are not enough words to express how proud of him I was for his accomplishments during basic training. I never doubted that he would excel; it was in his nature. He had to be the best at whatever he set his mind to conquer. We found strength and encouragement by assuring each other that it was only a short time before we would be together again.

Scott wrote every day, sometimes several times a day. He would explain everything he was learning so I would know what to expect since he was two weeks ahead of me. His letters were full of stories about the people in his platoon. Having never met them, I still felt as though I knew each one of them. Some of the stories made me laugh until I cried, and others made me sympathize with the unfortunate soldier who had become a teaching aid. Everyone wanted to avoid drawing any attention or being a teaching aid. We never wanted to make eye contact with a drill sergeant when answering. If we happened to make that mistake, the drill sergeant would be in our faces while screaming at us for eyeballing him, which resulted in push-ups.

The drill sergeants loved to say, "Drop and give me twenty." They always refer to their grandmothers when we did something wrong. If we only did fifteen push-ups, the drill sergeant's grandmother could do fifty in her sleep.

A calamitous event occurred near the end of Scott's basic training; he developed a staph infection. During a five-mile road march, a blister began to form on one of his heels. Although he did everything he had learned by cleaning the area, changing his socks, and rotating between both pairs of boots, the blister became infected anyway. The infection was so bad that he had to spend several days in the hospital. It was lanced, and a syringe was used to draw the infection out several times a day. It was packed with fresh gauze and antibiotics to fight the infection. Because he could not finish the final phase, he did not graduate with his class. He was upset and angry at having to go through basic all over again, but he accepted that it was what he had to do for our dreams to come true. He was always the protagonist!

Scott completed basic training at the top of his class for the second time and went on to Fort Sam Houston in San Antonio for Advanced Individual Training. He was training to be an operating room technician and had dreams of going to college, Officer Candidate School, and medical school. He wanted to become a brain surgeon.

When I stepped off the bus for basic training, I was instantly faced with a screaming drill sergeant who terrified me more than my father ever had. At that moment, my first instinct was to turn around, get right back on that bus, and go home. However, hearing my father's words inside my head telling me that I would never make it through basic training or amount to anything, I put one foot in front of the other and did as the screaming drill sergeant instructed.

During the first few weeks, everything we did was wrong—even if it was correct. I would drop and do twenty push-ups when I was in the wrong; at times, everyone had to drop for someone else's infraction. A drill sergeant's job is to turn a civilian into a soldier; in doing so, they take the "false confidence" you believed in when you enlisted and slowly break you down. However, at the same time, they are shaping you into a soldier who "knows" you have confidence for the rest of your life.

Our company had two extraordinary drill sergeants, although we did not think so at the time. Drill Sergeant Pallard and Drill Sergeant Kazak taught us and trained us to be more than we ever imagined was possible. They taught us to be ethical; being a soldier meant having morals and living by those morals in daily life and decisions.

Stepping off that bus and meeting the drill sergeant was one of the most conflicting experiences I have ever endured. I wanted to be there to improve my life, but I was terrified and just wanted to be back home. I am grateful for having been transformed into a soldier by two honorable, dedicated, caring military men. Those two drill sergeants are what the military is all about—honor, courage, commitment, integrity first, and service before self.

Promotion to platoon leader was a great achievement. I hated doing any type of physical fitness and was forever being yelled at when my hair fell below my collar. Every morning, it started out in a ponytail. I pinned it into a bun under my headgear. By midmorning, without fail, my hair would escape the bun and find its way below my collar. This was the routine for a couple of weeks, but after spending the majority of the days dropping for push-ups, I chopped it so short that there was no more worrying about it falling below my collar.

Under their training, guidance, and encouragement, I became a soldier—and a strong, confident young woman. I still carry those lessons with me and would not be who I am today had I not experienced life in the army.

I was a prissy girl who could not even make it a block on the first physical fitness run without feeling like my lungs were going to explode and I just wanted to go home. I could not do a single push-up or sit-up, but they never gave up on me. They never allowed me to give up, regardless of how many times I wanted to. They knew something about me that I didn't know, I could do it!

Mental strength, physical endurance, firing and cleaning weapons, and throwing hand grenades were some of the skills that transformed me into a soldier. The lessons were taught and learned with blood, sweat, and tears. When it was our platoon's time for the firing range, I was not wearing glasses because I was too cute to wear the military-issued glasses, which were known as "birth control glasses" because no one wearing them had ever been known to get lucky.

During qualifying, the drill sergeant screamed, "Private, what in the hell are you firing at?"

I said, "The target."

My "buddy" ratted me out when she asked where my glasses were. Doing push-ups until you can do no more and then having to do more was a bitch. The next day, I had to re-qualify. I wore the birth control glasses and aimed more proficiently. The sacrifice was worth it when I earned the sharpshooter badge with the M16A1 rifle and the expert badge with the hand grenade. From that day on, wearing those glasses became essential if surviving basic was a goal. Scott and Brandon were a little miffed that I had scored better than both of them, and I loved to remind them of it as often as I could.

During land navigation and map reading, we were taught the basic colors of a map, what each color represented, what the military symbols meant, where the legend of the map was found, what contour lines were, three types of contour lines, how many miles are in one degree, and how many North's there are on a military map. These represent just a small portion of land and map reading training. We also learned to read a map and use reference points to navigate from point A to point B.

There was one small problem: no matter how much they went over it, it just did not click. Pretending to know how to accomplish this task while not understanding how to read the map was worrisome. However, telling the drill sergeants was not an option; in hindsight, that could have been a grave mistake. When it was my group's turn, we went off into the woods with the coordinates that would take us to point A where we would find a clue that would lead us to point B. That clue would lead back to camp, but it just did not work for me.

After walking circles for what seemed like hours, a road came into view. Common sense implied that following the road would lead to the campsite. However, common sense did not win this time. Three miles from our training area, another training company drill sergeant discovered a lost soldier walking down the dirt road without a care in the world. If having a drill sergeant screaming at you is terrifying enough, try being screamed at by a total stranger who found you just as you were about to walk into a live fire area. Any soldier who did not pass the task involuntary stayed up most of night while the drill sergeant explained land navigation and map reading every way he knew how. It took a while, but I finally got it.

We also trained to use chemical masks during nuclear, biological, or chemical attacks, along with defending your position and tracking your enemy, landmine defense, and rappelling at the confidence tower. We were trained to be soldiers, and they taught us army heritage and the seven army core values. They trained us to be all we could be and to live by the soldier's creed.

Soldier's Creed

I am an American soldier.

I am a warrior and a member of a team.

I serve the people of the United States, and live the army's values.

I will always place the mission first.

I will never accept defeat.

I will never quit.

I will never leave a fallen comrade.

I am disciplined, physically and mentally tough, trained, and

Proficient in my warrior tasks and drills.

I always maintain my arms, my equipment, and myself.

I am an expert, and I am a professional.

I stand ready to deploy, engage, and destroy the enemies of

The United States of America in close combat.

I am a guardian of freedom and the American way of life.

I am an American soldier.

During the last phase of basic training, we had to pass a final physical fitness test. This was a problem because I had injured my ankle during the obstacle course. "The Weaver" was a twelve-foot A-frame-shaped wall made out of railroad ties that were spaced so that we could weave under one and over the other. With an air of confidence, we began to weave our bodies over and under the boards, working our way to the top. At the top, we reversed our weaving while working back toward the ground. On the descent, my foot slipped, and I fell from the top. I dislocated my hip and fractured my right ankle. Prior to my injury, a drill sergeant who was demonstrating on the obstacle course fractured his ribs, and within minutes of my injury, a soldier on the Warrior Tower was seriously injured, shutting the course down for the remainder of the day.

At the emergency room, they rotated my hip into place and encased my foot in a plaster cast. After being released from the emergency room, I awkwardly hobbled outside on crutches. I was wondering how to get back to the barracks. It was a long walk on a normal day, but it was not a normal day. There was no way to hobble that far without causing further injuries. Another possibility was calling the company to see if arrangements for transportation were possible. Since I was not brave enough to do that, a cab was the only remaining option. While trying to make a plan of action, a cab pulled up. When a soldier emerged from the back seat, my plan was set in motion. After waving to the cabbie and managing to half-wobble, half-walk over, I inquired about the cost for a ride to the barracks. I was overwhelmed with relief when he quoted a reasonable price.

As the cab pulled up to the barracks, evening formation had just been dismissed. Since it was the weekend, we were given time off, allowing an opportunity to keep my foot elevated. However, while trying to do what the emergency room doctor had instructed, time seemed to crawl by. Any other time, hanging around in your bunk would have been an answered prayer, but it was the weekend. That meant going to the base store. Life sucked, or so it seemed.

On Monday, it was back to business as usual. We had one task left in order to complete basic training; we had to take our final physical fitness test. In order to graduate, I had to pass with a score of 150 or better.

Taking the final physical fitness test in a cast was not possible. Cautiously approaching the drill sergeant, I asked if I would be allowed to graduate with my class. Thinking about what Scott had gone through; I was terrified about the drill sergeant's response. However, he said it was not his decision; it would be up to First Sergeant O'Shea. There was no possibility that First Sergeant would waive the final physical fitness test requirement. The sweat and tears over the last eight weeks had been for nothing!

Later in the day, Drill Sergeant Pallard said that First Sergeant O'Shea would hold me back to be recycled if I could not complete the required physical fitness test. Feeling devastated and hopeless, I made up my mind that I would not be held back. There was no way in hell I would be repeating the eight weeks of hell the army calls basic training. I would take that final physical fitness test and pass it—even if it killed me! Better to be dead than to relive the last eight weeks.

After morning formation the following day, I requested permission to go to sick call. Drill Sergeant Pallard asked why. I leaned heavily on the crutches while attempting to mimic being in pain. I lied to him and claimed that my ankle was radiating with pain. In no time, I was riding in a cab; however, this time I was heading to the base hospital.

After finding the emergency room, the search for the doctor ensued. Once he had been located, I attempted to persuade him to cut the cast off. When he wanted to know why, my answer was simple. I said, "Because I am going to take my final physical fitness test."

He did not like that idea at all and advised against it. However, after several minutes of going back and forth, he conceded. He explained that a waiver of release would need to be signed and placed in the official medical records in order to remove the cast.

I could not sign my John Hancock on that form fast enough; true to his word, the cast came off as soon as it was signed. Wishing me good luck, he sent some ace bandages, pain medication, and instructions to keep it elevated with an ice pack on it as much as possible to keep the swelling down.

Following the doctor's orders, I kept it elevated for the rest of that day and night while alternating from an ice pack to a heating pad and praying I could pull it off. The next morning, after wrapping it with sports tape and an ace wrap, just as the doctor had instructed, it would not fit in the tennis shoe. I could not believe my dreams were being dashed because of a small shoe, and I was ready to quit. When Drill Sergeant Pallard heard, he went to his locker and brought one of his tennis shoes. It was a perfect fit!

While experiencing some of the worst pain ever, I still completed the final physical fitness test. Over the years, I have often wondered if I would have completed the run had it not been for the encouragement of a fellow soldier who volunteered to run the two miles with me. Thanks to her selfless act and encouragement, we completed the run, finishing with the best two-mile time up to that point. After enduring so much to complete the basic training requirements, First Sergeant O'Shea, citing a safety hazard, would not allow me to participate in the graduation ceremony. His decision was devastating after all the hell I had endured, but I had no choice but to comply. At that point, all that mattered was graduating.

It was with elation and excitement that we began the next phase of army training. Advanced Individual Training—or AIT as the military referred to it—was also known as Military Occupation Specialties training or MOS. The transportation specialist program was a seven-week course at an army base in Virginia. We were looking forward to Advanced Individual Training because we heard it was a more relaxed atmosphere than basic training had been—and it came with more privileges. It definitely was different. In basic training, females were in an all-female dorm, and it was shocking to know that we were to be in the same dorm as the males. However, the females were on one half, and the males were on the other. We remained separated into our own platoons.

After a day to settle into our new dorms, we were marched to the supply building to have our gear issued. Our drill sergeant left us at parade rest and went inside to see if they were ready for our platoon. While we waited, we broke off into small groups, talking and enjoying the relaxed atmosphere. It amazed us how differently soldiers who had graduated basic training were treated. We could actually stand around and talk without fear of being dropped for "twenty." Enjoying our new freedom, we shared stories about life prior to the army and laughed. One of the male drill sergeants approached our group and yelled, "Private, front and center." He meant, "Get your ass over here now!"

While running to where he was standing, I was trying to remember what wrongdoing I could have committed. When I stopped and came to attention in front of him, nothing came to mind. However, training had taught us that we were in deep shit if any drill sergeant other than our own called us out.

I was standing at attention, waiting to be dressed down or even punished, but he asked me where I was from. *What? Surely, that was not what he had asked. Why would he need to know that?*

Still standing at attention, I quickly replied, "Texas, drill sergeant."

He said, "I thought so by your accent. I heard you talking earlier and wondered if you were."

Still scared and wondering what he wanted, I continued to stand at attention, waiting.

Without any warning or provocation, he leaned in and whispered, "I love your accent."

I was stunned. I did not know what to think or say—or even if a reply was expected. My internal alarms warned me to turn and run; however, we had been taught not to question or contradict those in authority or higher rank. I just stood there, speechless.

When our drill sergeant came outside and noticed one of the male platoon's drill sergeants talking to one of his recruits, he screamed to get with our platoon. While running back to the platoon, he called us into formation and marched us into the supply warehouse. We spent the rest of that afternoon having our field gear issued to us. Once every soldier was processed, we marched to our barracks and spent the evening organizing and correctly packing it into our duffel bags.

With all the commotion that day, what the drill sergeant had said was totally forgotten. Our training in our military occupational specialty had officially started, and we were getting as settled into life at our AIT as a soldier can. During AIT, we learned the skills to perform our army jobs.

At one of many diverse AIT schools, we received hands-on training and field instruction to make us experts in a specific career field. We also gained the discipline and work ethic to help us in any path of life.

The military occupation I had selected was transportation management coordinator (88N). My job was to keep the army on the move. Our school's motto is *"Per Scientiam Progredimur* (Through learning, we progress)." During AIT, we learned how to operate and maintain army tactical trucks, material-handling equipment, and watercraft. The training occurred on state-of-the-art simulation and training facilities. We learned about transportation operations, traffic management, convoy operations, cargo transfer, cargo documentation, movement control, operation of heavy material-handling equipment, sailing and maintenance of army vessels, and unloading aircraft, ships, railcars, and trucks.

Transportation management coordinators were primarily responsible for scheduling and selecting the modes of transportation for personnel and equipment. They organized, planned, and oversaw the movement of vehicles, personnel, and cargo worldwide

During morning mail, Private Dunn boomed through the room. I jumped up with elation when another letter from Scott arrived. It was so exciting hearing from Scott. With a controlled eagerness, I would slowly open the letter and excitedly read all about his training adventures at Fort Sam Houston. We wrote to each other as often as we could and shared what our posts, platoons, and fellow soldiers were like.

Approximately a week after receiving our gear, I was reading a letter in my dorm room. A knock on the door interrupted me. Our door was open, and a roommate called for the soldier to enter. As she walked in, she asked which one of us was Private Dunn. She handed me a piece of paper that instructed me to report to First Sergeant Higgans's office at 20:00 hours.

After reading the note, my roommates wanted to know what was going on. I often turned to them for advice and guidance and did so again because they had arrived several weeks ahead of our training class. They knew how things were done in our company. They said not to worry about it because if it were something serious, our platoon's drill sergeant would have been the one to issue the command.

After placing the note on the bed, trying not to worry, I returned to Scott's letter. It did not work because I could only focus on the note— and what it meant. That night, I tossed and turned throughout the night, wondering what the First Sergeant could possibly need to see me about. I was pretty positive I had not done anything to be in trouble. Why was I being summoned to his office? It was a long, restless night, and I was still stressing in the morning.

That evening after chow and the final formation for that day, I reluctantly headed to First Sergeant Higgans's office. I was terrified and shaking all the way down to my combat boots because our training had taught us that there was only one reason to be summoned to the first sergeant's office. My ass was grass. The closer to his office, the more my legs felt like spaghetti. A hundred pounds of weights weighed down each step, and my heart raced so fast that I could hear it pounding in my ears. My hands were sweaty and clammy, and I wanted to be anywhere else.

Part of the reason for being worried was that we had heard one of the male platoon's drill sergeants had been appointed as our new first sergeant. Rumors were flying around as to what happened to cause our first sergeant to leave, but we soon found out that he had been arrested on charges of rape.

Not knowing whom our new first sergeant was led to even more anxiety because the only interaction with our former first sergeant had been friendly. He would often stop to talk to the soldiers. He would inquire about our training and if we had settled into life as a soldier. In addition, to let us know that he was there if the soldiers ever needed anything. After basic training, his friendliness with the troops was reassuring because we were still questioning whether we had made the right decision about joining.

With a churning and turning stomach, the journey continued down that long hallway, dreading every step. Opening the door to the clerk's office with shaking, sweating hands and walking into the outer office, it was clear that the company's clerks had gone for the evening. Timidly and apprehensively, after approaching the door and knocking, my wait began. After a minute or so, he issued the command to enter. Upon entering his office, just as we had been trained to do in basic, I came to a stop and instantly moved into the position of attention. He looked up, gave the command for parade rest. To say it was shocking to see the same drill sergeant who had questioned me the day our equipment had been issued would be putting it mildly. Those internal alarms that warn you of danger sounded like a war zone going off.

He must have seen the shock because he asked how I was adapting to my Advanced Individual training.

I replied, "I am doing fine, First Sergeant Higgans. I am looking forward to graduating and being assigned to my first duty station so my husband and I will be together again."

He said that he had noticed my relationship status—married to another soldier—while reviewing the company records. "He's at Fort Sam Houston, correct?"

"Yes, First Sergeant. He is training as an operating room technician."

First Sergeant Higgans stood up and approached while handing me a piece of paper. The slip of paper had a room number and time written on it. He instructed me to report for duty as indicated and to wear PT gear, which were shorts and a T-shirt. First Sergeant turned away and dismissed me.

After returning to the dorm room, my roommates wanted to know what First Sergeant Higgans wanted. When I told them that he had assigned me to duty in a couple of hours and showed them the paper he had given me, they looked at each other and smiled, but they said nothing else before they left to go to the Post Exchange. Determined not to worry, I picked up the letter from my husband and continued reading where I had left off. I was trying to finish it and hoped to have enough time to write back before reporting for duty. After finishing the letter, I realized it was almost time to report. After addressing the envelope and hurriedly heading to the mailroom, I was surprised to see the room number was only two doors down from our dorm room.

After dropping off the letter in the mailroom and checking in with the duty sergeant—not daring to be late—I hurried to the room with the note in my hand. Upon arriving at the assigned door, it was still closed. I was sure it would have been open by the time I returned from the mailroom. I knocked on the door and waited for a reply. I looked down at the paper to confirm that it was the correct room.

I knocked on the door again and waited. When there was no reply, I turned the knob to see if the door would open. It opened into a room black as a moonless night. While reaching inside the room and feeling for a light switch, I was suddenly pulled into the room and a hand was placed over my mouth. Before my natural instincts could kick in, a man was pushing me against a cold, hard brick wall. There was no doubt that it was a man since a hard appendage pressed against me.

My first reaction was to fight him off, but he was so much stronger. No matter how hard I fought and struggled, I could not push him away. The more I fought, the harder he pressed me into the wall. Once he had had enough, he said that if I continued to fight him, I was going to get hurt. He said he did not want to hurt me; he just wanted to get to know me better. He began telling about how he could not stop thinking about me and how much he loved the sound of my Southern accent. As soon as he said that, I knew who had pinned me against the wall.

There are not enough words to completely describe the terror I was suddenly overwhelmed by. However, it is my intent to help you understand what I felt that night as much as possible. Close your eyes and travel back to a time when your heart almost stopped beating because you were so scared—maybe it was being lost as a child, your first wreck, or maybe your first speeding ticket. Now multiply that feeling by 1,000 percent, and you have a small glimmer into my fear.

I was so confused. Why was First Sergeant Higgans doing this? He told me not to fight him because he would make my life a living hell. He went on to say that my husband and I would never serve at the same base. Being new to the army, I had no idea that he did not have that kind of power. With my mind racing as fast as my heart was pounding, I listened to him tell me that we were going to become very good friends.

All soldiers take an oath to "obey the orders of the president of the United States and the orders of the officers appointed over me, according to regulations and the Uniform Code of Military Justice. So help me God." From my first day as a recruit, I was taught that the only way to survive was through obedience and fear. I learned to view my superior officers and non-commissioned officers as God and to obey and fear them. We did not question them. We did as we were told—period! Because of the obedience and fear of our superiors that were beaten into us—along with simply being terrified—I did not fight him again.

He pushed me onto a cot in a corner of the room and removed my clothing. I heard claps of thunder and saw streaks of lightning through a small dark window while he raped me. As he raped me, he would ask questions and demand that I respond so he could hear my Southern accent or my "sexy voice" as he referred to it. When he was not forcing me talk to him, he was telling how much he was looking forward to us becoming very special friends. He whispered into my ear about how his thoughts had been consumed by me since the first time he had heard my voice. This went on for hours—or at least that was what it felt like. When he finished, he told me to wait fifteen minutes before leaving the room. He looked into my eyes and said he could not wait to make love to me again.

I curled into the fetal position on the cot and began to shake and sob uncontrollably. I'm not sure how long I cried, but I finally got up, dressed, and ran back to the shelter of my dorm room. Entering the room, I was thankful to find my roommates were still gone. After turning the shower on as hot as it would go and stripping out of those clothes, I stepped into the scalding water and stood there shaking. It seemed as if hours had passed while I waited for the hot water to wash away the feel and smell of him. At the same time, I scrubbed until my skin felt raw. I attempted to wash the filth off of me as I stood there sobbing. Somehow, I managed to get out of the shower, got dressed, and collapsed onto my bunk. I cried myself to sleep.

My first thought was how I was going to tell my husband about being raped. When I did, what would he say? Would it change how he felt about us? My next thought was that I could never tell him because First Sergeant Higgans had said he would make sure we never served together. Not sure about what to do, I avoided Scott's calls for the next several days because I was afraid to talk to him. I knew if we talked, I would tell him about being raped. However, at the same time, I was also terrified of not telling him. That all changed when First Sergeant Higgans raped me again. I knew without a doubt that I had to tell my husband.

Scott was the only person who knew about the rapes and the threats. I wanted to report him and believed with all my heart that my husband would want me to do so as well. I expected him to be angry. I wanted him to do something about it, but he told me not to say anything because First Sergeant Higgans could ruin our army careers and our dreams for our future. I felt hurt and abandoned by his response, and the rapes went unreported—just as Scott had said. What happened to the knight in shining armor I married? Where was the man who had sworn to protect me? I had never felt as utterly alone as I did at the end of that phone call.

The rapes continued during the seven weeks of our training course. Suffering in silence, I began to hate my husband, the army, and myself. I was in constant fear and on alert. I never knew when or where it was going to happen again. At times, a soldier would bring a note with a message to report to the storage room where the first rape had occurred. At other times, it would happen late at night while on fire watch—at any moment and any location. Several times after entering the female latrine to perform fireguard duties, he would walk out of a stall and pull me into his arms as if we were lovers. He would reach into a stall, retrieve a sleeping bag, and rape me on the bathroom floor. His favorite spot was his office with only the dim glow of a lamp and the soft sound of music.

He would often ask how making love to a real man felt compared to a boy. He wanted to know if I would miss what it felt like to be held by a real man when I was in the arms of a boy. He made the same comments each time. He often made me read a book so he could hear my voice—or my accent. At times, that was all he wanted, but at other times, he would just rape me on his office floor. In hindsight, I believe he got a thrill out of knowing there were non-commissioned officers and soldiers all around, and he could do whatever he wanted without any fear of being caught or stopped.

I was living in constant fear. I never knew when or where he was going to be waiting—or when and where I was going to be raped again. I went to bed terrified and woke up terrified. It started to take a toll on me; my mind and body longed for sleep but dreaded it at the same time. Nightmares had become reality, and reality had become nightmares; there was no escape from it.

I was jumping at every little noise; my nerves were shot from being on constant guard. Even fellow soldiers noticed the changes. One evening while walking to the Post Exchange, a fellow soldier from the platoon commented on my jumpiness. She suggested that I try smoking. She said that she smoked because it helped settle her nerves. She handed me a Virginia Slims; although I became nauseous, it helped my nerves. It did not take long to discover that it did not help the lungs, which was evident during my next physical fitness test. Thank God that habit only lasted three weeks!

I Lost My Life to Fear

Fear in the midst of the night

Fear in broad daylight

Fear of what could happen

Fear of what did happen

Fear insinuating my every day

Fear controlling all that I say

Fear governing me as I sleep

Fear deriding me as I weep

Fear that puts my sanity at stake

Fear that prays for me to break

Fear that strikes me with perplexity

Fear with a recipe of complexity

Fear that deprived me of exhilaration

Fear that admitted me to frustration

Fear that is prevailing my mind

Fear that manipulates humankind

Fear that still holds my life today

The stress and fear was affecting me mentally and physically; my stomach started to hurt all the time. I was clenching and grinding my teeth so hard that my teeth, jaws, and head would hurt all the time. Around the fourth week of training, during a weekend pass, some of the soldiers rented a couple of rooms just outside of the base and threw a party. When I arrived, the party was already in full swing. Someone was handing out drinks as we entered. After a little while, I slowly started to relax for the first time in weeks. Since I was not a drinker and was not there to hook up—as most of the other soldiers were—I was ready to head back to the dorms after an hour or so.

After saying good-bye to my friends, I began the walk back toward the base. I had just made it out of the hotel parking lot when a truck pulled up in front of me and blocked my path. *Oh God, I am going to be kidnapped.* When the window rolled down, it was First Sergeant Higgans. He said to keep quiet and get in the truck. I do not know why I did not scream or run, but I was terrified of him.

Doing as he said, I got in without causing a scene. He drove around the building to a room he had rented. He had candles burning and low music playing in the background; he said we could finally make love as he had dreamed of doing from the first moment he heard my voice. Over the next several hours, I was repeatedly raped as he taunted me about being with a real man versus a boy. After what felt like days, he told me to get dressed and go back to the dorms. After forcing a kiss, he said he had really enjoyed our evening,. I jumped up and threw my clothes on as fast as possible; I just wanted to get the hell out of that room and away from him. I hated him more than words could ever express.

While walking back to base, sobbing uncontrollably, a male soldier caught up and asked if I was okay. I was not about to tell him what had happened! The first sergeant's threats were always on my mind. I lied and said my husband and I'd had a fight, and I was just trying to get back to the dorms. As we were walking, I doubled over in pain and started throwing up bright red blood.

The soldier told me to stay there because he was going to run to the guard shack to get help. He asked the military police to call for an ambulance. I was still throwing up blood when the ambulance arrived. I was taken to the base hospital, and after a few hours and several tests, I was diagnosed with a bleeding peptic ulcer. I was admitted for two days and then released to return to my company. They prescribed medication for the ulcer and gave instructions to reduce stress.

I wanted to scream, "What a joke!" Instead, I just said I would do my best. During my short time at Fort Eustis, I had developed temporomandibular joint disorder, more often referred to as TMJ, from clenching my jaws and grinding my teeth. I was performing poorly in my training classes because I just wanted to finish training and leave my hell on earth.

It felt as if time had stopped. Twenty-four hours felt more like a week. As we began to prepare for field maneuvers, I craved the training that most others dreaded. During our fifth week of training, we went into the field for a week. I was excited and had been looking forward to it for weeks because I would have a reprieve without being raped or being in constant fear. However, I was proven wrong.

On the morning we were to march out to our location, I had a dental appointment and would join my company in the field. After getting a filling and listening to the dentist's lecture about grinding my teeth and the damage it caused—along with another warning to reduce my stress, which made me want to laugh at the irony—I left for the field. After arriving and noticing a section of tents, I asked another soldier if she knew where the additional tents were since I needed to set mine up.

She explained that the tents had been set up already and pointed to a row of tents. "Yours is all the way at the end—just where we were instructed to put it." She started laughing as she walked over to a group of soldiers.

I was puzzled by her comment and did not understand it, but I shook it off while trying to locate my platoon for the remaining exercises.

During our evening formation, prior to being released to go to our tents, one of the drill sergeants gave instructions that we were not to sleep in our battle dress uniforms. They would be conducting a tent-by-tent inspection to make sure that everyone was complying.

One of the soldiers asked precisely what the rest of us was wondering, how he would know what we were sleeping in.

The drill sergeant explained that a tent check would be conducted nightly. When a drill sergeant came to our tent and announced himself or herself, we were to show them a leg up to the thigh.

I could not help but wonder who my tent mate would be as I walked toward my tent. However, upon entering the tent and seeing that the only gear inside belonged to me, my stomach instantly turned sour because my fears were now confirmed. I knew what was going to happen. I did not want to go in there. I just wanted to leave and go back home to Texas.

As I stood there debating what to do, First Sergeant Higgans walked up behind me and informed me that since I was the odd female out, he had set up my tent for me.

I said, "Thank you, First Sergeant Higgans." However, I really wanted to scream at the top of my lungs.

Before he turned to walk off, he leaned in and whispered, "I hope you appreciate what I have done for you."

At that moment, it became clear that the week of reprieve I craved and prayed for was not going to happen. The living hell had followed me to the field. I wondered why. *What happened that I deserve to live through this?*

Later that night, I heard First Sergeant announce, "Tent inspection." The flap opened, and he instructed me to open my sleeping bag in order to confirm I was not in my battle dress uniform. While standing there and leering, he said, "See you in a little while, beautiful."

As soon as he left, I dashed out of my tent and had just enough time to make it to the port-a-potty before throwing up my dinner rations. He brazenly raped me in that tent in middle of the woods with fellow soldiers and non-commissioned officers surrounding us. They knew and did nothing! How could this be happening when the army's values were supposed to be loyalty, duty, respect, selfless service, honor, integrity, and personal courage? Where were the leaders whose jobs were to train, mold, and protect fellow soldiers? This was not the army in which I had enlisted!

Every evening someone was assigned fireguard duty, which is similar to a security guard's job. The job was to ensure that everyone was in his or her tents and accounted for along with patrolling the area surrounding the tented area. On the evening I was assigned fireguard duty, I went to find the soldier I was to replace. As he was turning over fireguard duty, he gave instructions to stay away from the last female's tent per the orders of First Sergeant Higgans. I was shocked and mortified to hear that he had given that order—and even more that not one of the soldiers or drill sergeants had done anything about it.

An institution like the military trains people to obey and not challenge, period! Being away from my family and in another state for the first time in my life, I did as I was told and remained silent. After all, Scott had compelled me to stay silent because, as he kept pointing out, it was only for a short time compared to the rest of our lives.

Because of the way he reacted when I told him about the initial rape, I never told him about the other rapes. I saw no point in it. I knew what he would say and do because he had already said and done it. I was expected to take one for the team.

Life Built on Hopes and Dreams

Life built on hopes and dreams

Not at all what it seems.

We plan, and we pray,

Trying to shape the clay.

Only to have it crack and shatter,

Wondering if it really matters.

Life is built on hopes and dreams

Fluttering away on a butterfly's wings.

Mapping out our lives day by day

Struggling to keep disappointments at bay.

Trying to keep our hopes and dreams from tatters,

Wondering if it really matters.

We began to argue and fight all the time. He could not—or did not want to—understand why I seemed angry all the time or why my letters were not filled with love and admiration as they once had been. He even had the nerve to accuse me of cheating on him since his calls were not answered or returned as often as he felt they should have been—or as they had been. We began to look at divorce as a solution for our problems. Nothing mattered any longer; it took every ounce of being just to survive on a daily basis. Life meant nothing at that point; my thoughts were more often than not filled with countless ways of ending this pain and to leaving the hell, life had become.

During our sixth week of training, First Sergeant Higgans summoned me to his office during normal working hours. Since this was so out of the norm, or what had become the norm, I was even more frightened. He informed me that the chaplain at Fort Sam Houston had contacted him with a request. He explained that Scott had spoken to his chaplain and had requested an emergency leave so that he could come in person and convince me that our marriage was worth fighting for. First Sergeant Higgans actually smiled while saying it, and then he informed me that I was being given a weekend pass to visit with my husband. If I knew what was best, I would see to it that he left a happy man.

When Scott arrived that weekend, doing as instructed, I reaffirmed our love and assured him that everything would be all right. I said I was having problems adjusting and was not dealing well with being away from home. When he left a happy man, I died a little more!

From that point on, every time First Sergeant Higgans raped me, he asked if I thought of him when Scott had made love to me that weekend. He often reminded me how much I would miss the feel of a real man's hands caressing my body. He wanted to know who was a better lover, and he laughed at my silence. He said that he could show my husband how a real man made love to a woman, and I could be his model since I was perfect for the part. The humiliation never stopped, and I began to hate everything—even myself—for being so weak.

When graduation date arrived, life felt as if it had a purpose again. The nightmares that had filled every waking and sleeping moment were finally going to end. Suicide was a prevailing thought, and I do not believe I could have endured one more day of his torture.

After graduation, we received our first duty station orders. I was elated to read I would be going to Fort Knox in Kentucky. It could have been the moon for all I cared—as long as it was not Fort Eustis. That bus could not pull out fast enough for me, and I left without even a backward glance. There was only one direction—forward.

When that bus passed through the gates, leaving only the shadows of Fort Eustis behind, I was determined to do the same. Everything that had occurred while I was there was buried in the far regions of my brain, never to be thought about again. At least, that was how it was supposed to be.

Our bus arrived at Fort Knox around midnight; when we managed to get to processing, there was just one sergeant on duty. He actually spoke to us like real people, like soldiers. Processing us one at a time, we produced our duty assignment orders, and then he confirmed the unit still had a need. If not, you were reassigned and your reassignment orders were issued.

When he noticed my orders were for an assignment to a field unit, he looked at me and said, "You are going to a new unit." He assigned me Company A 1st Battalion as a transportation clerk. This was the beginning I was looking forward to, a new start. I was hoping to settle in and put everything in the past, but it was not a very successful attempt.

After having nightmares most nights, always being on alert for something bad to happen, and staying in the dorm room when not working, isolation was to be my savior. However, the walls started closing in, and even the sense of safety was gone.

One weekend, some of the soldiers were watching football or shooting pool in the dayroom. My roommate was pleading with me to leave the room. I had not been out of my room for weeks other than to work, and I gave in. We were playing a round of pool when some other soldiers came in and started watching the game. They offered us drinks, but I declined.

As we were about to head back to our pool game, my roommate leaned over and whispered, "It will help you sleep better." She handed me her drink. Sipping on the drink as she waited for them to make her another one, I decided it was not that bad. As we continued our pool game, the drink had its desired effect. I was calmer—until the room was called to attention. Whenever a senior enlisted or officer walked into a room, everyone had to stand and come to the position of attention. First Sergeant Davis had walked in.

After telling us to stand down or continue as we were, he walked over to the group watching the football game and chatted with them for a bit. They continued to shout and cheer on the teams, whooping and yelling for touchdowns. I continued shooting pool, talking and actually had forgotten he was there—until he walked over to us and asked how the game was going. We told him it was a close game and asked if he would like to join us. He said he had to run, but he just wanted to stop in and check in on his troops. And then, he asked he asked to see our identification cards.

Oh man, this is not good. I am underage and drinking. We handed over our identification. When he looked at them, he inquired about how long I had been in the unit.

I replied, "Only for a couple of weeks, maybe a month, First Sergeant Davis."

He handed our identification back, took the drink I was holding, and said he would see me at 0800 hours in the morning in his office. *Why does this keep happening? All I want is to feel normal again. Is that too much to ask?*

I did not sleep that night because I did not want to go to his office as I had been instructed. I knew what was going to happen; I had already lived through it for seven weeks during AIT.

At 0750, I was dressed and standing outside his door. I was so nervous that I thought I was going to pass out or be sick. At 0800, I was summoned into the office and was surprised and relieved to see my platoon sergeant in there as well.

I was ordered to parade rest, a relaxed position of attention, and First Sergeant Davis asked if I knew why he had requested to see me.

I replied, "Yes, First Sergeant. I was drinking, and I am underage."

He nodded and asked how often I drank.

I said, "I do not drink, First Sergeant. I just have not been sleeping well, and I thought it would help me."

He asked if there was anything they could do to help.

Not wanting to draw any more attention, I lied and said I was just having a hard time adjusting to being away from my husband and home.

He listened to the story I had rehearsed, and then he explained the infractions that I could be punished for. His next statement was a shocker. He said, "Private Dunn, you seem like a good kid. Your platoon sergeant said you have been an exceptional soldier. You arrive early and leave late. He also said you have not been in any other trouble. I have decided that we will put a letter of reprimand in your file and assign you to volunteer with the chaplain every Wednesday for the next month."

I served the punishment, and I enjoyed it so much that I continued to volunteer for the next year. The chaplain said he could see a broken soul in my eyes the first time we met. We talked often, and through his kindness, life began to find a balance again. On several occasions, I almost shared the rapes with the chaplain, but the nightmares had almost gone away. Scott and I were working on our marriage, and I decided they were best left in the past. They just needed to remain buried where they could no longer hurt. I started putting the horrors of the last few months behind me as if they had never happened. I was moving forward, when once again, I lost my faith in the army.

While working with the chaplain, there was a young girl who would come on Wednesday for piano lessons. When she arrived early or had to wait for her ride, we would sit and talk. During one of our conversations, she asked if she could tell a secret. I had to cross my heart and stick a pin in my eye that I would keep her secret. I instantly agreed to do so; after all, it was just an eight-year-old child's secret. Surely I could keep it, right?

Wrong! She confided that her dad, one of the base commanders, made her play a game she did not like. She explained the rules. He would touch her in her no-no areas, and then she had to touch his no-no area. Then, she said he would kiss her there, and it felt funny. When she tried to make him stop, he would get mad at her. She described having to kiss his no-no area, which made her sick.

Listening to her, I wanted to throw up as anger and rage filled me to the bones. What was wrong with the world? With my heart breaking, she told the last part of the game. She had to bounce up and down on his lap with her panties off. She crumpled into my arms in tears, asking if she could please go home with me. I explained that she could not go home with me, but I would make sure she never had to play that game again.

As soon as she left the church, I immediately found the chaplain. He was talking to some of the soldiers picking up their children. Upon seeing my ashen face and shaking hands, he could tell I was in distress. He ushered me quickly into his office. I was shaking and crying as I betrayed her confidence and relayed her secret, just as she had told it. The chaplain assured me that he would take care of it. He told me that I did not have to worry about it anymore, but I was worried about that beautiful little girl who was being abused.

When she did not show for her piano lessons the following week, worry overwhelmed me. After all of the students had been picked up that evening, I asked the chaplain if he knew why she was not there.

He said she was sick and would be there the next Wednesday as usual. When she was not there the next week, I again asked about her.

The chaplain said they'd had a family emergency and had gone out of town, but she would be there next week. He told me not to worry because everything was okay. He had spoken to her parents.

On the third Wednesday, she still did not return for her lessons. I made a comment about going to visit her to the chaplain and was floored when he turned to me and said, "She is not there. They were transferred to another base last week. As he turned to walk away, the chaplain said, "Just let it go, Private Dunn."

I could not let it go, and I never stepped foot in that chapel again. I never stopped worrying about that little girl either. Twenty-seven years later, the guilt is still overpowering. I still wonder what—if anything—could have been handled differently in order to help her instead of fail her.

I settled into my job, and I was excelling at it. As a result, I was beginning to regain some confidence in myself. As a transportation specialist, my responsibility was making all travel arrangements for any military members on the base who were traveling on Permanent Change of Station (PCS) orders or Temporary Duty Orders (TDY).

The busy, hectic pace kept my mind busy, and a busy mind did not have time to think. Reservations were constantly being made and then remade due to some minor or major changes that always seemed to happen at the last minute. When others complained about the frequent changes, I would offer to take over. I loved the challenge—anything to fill the time and keep busy until quitting time.

Supervisors gloated over my dedication and sheer determination; if only they knew it was how I was surviving the demons in my head. Grateful officers, non-commissioned officers, enlisted soldiers, and family members wrote letters of accommodations for above the call of duty dedication and perseverance. I was almost beginning to feel normal again.

Scott finished his AIT at Fort Sam Houston and then transferred to Fort Riley for his on-the-job training. I was not happy about this and did not understand why he could not do his training at Ireland

Army Hospital at Fort Knox where I was stationed and waiting for him. Knowing there was no choice, we continued to write and call often, still hoping to make our marriage work. It was difficult at times because of the distance. Many times, I just needed him to say he was sorry for not supporting me and for not defending our marriage. I missed him holding me in his arms.

When his training was completed, he received his PCS orders for Ireland Army Hospital. We were going to be stationed together! All the sacrifices were finally worth it. Once he arrived, we began to attend counseling with one of the post chaplains. Let me make it very clear that it was not the same chaplain who sold that little girl out. We remained married, but our relationship was never the same.

The innocent blind love of teenagers was forever lost to us. At times, we stayed together because it was easier than divorcing—or that is what I believed at the time. Scott began to cover extra shifts when he was not training for marathons. He often said that staying away was better than fighting all the time. To cope with everything that was out of control in our lives, I became a perfectionist and a control freak. I had every minute detail of our lives planned out, and if something did not happen the way I had it planned, I would have a meltdown. World War III was in full-force mode. Nothing seemed to change; the more

I tried to be perfect, the more miserable our lives became. We were married strangers living under the same roof, but neither of us was strong enough to leave.

At work, those traits worked in my favor. As a result, I was presented with several accommodations and letters of praise. I was promoted to specialist, but in my mind, I was never good enough. I would always be the poor, pathetic girl who was being raped without anyone caring enough to do anything about it. The more praise I received, the more incompetent I felt. It was as if I was living with two people trapped inside—the perfectionist and the failure—and they were always battling for the lead position. Where one excelled at work, the other withdrew deeper into its wall of safety at home, cutting a deeper wedge than the day before and growing in size and depth.

Eventually, things began to improve between us. In 1987, I became pregnant, and we started rebuilding our lives. We decided to have a baby, but, after just three months, we decided to wait a while longer. However, three weeks after we changed our minds, I was taking my physical fitness test and began to cramp in the abdominal and pelvic area. After completing the physical fitness test, I returned home to shower and dress for work. While undressing, I noticed I was spotting. I had just had a period a couple of weeks ago, which concerned me.

On my way to work, I stopped by the base clinic and signed in to have it checked. When the doctor came in and read over the chart, he dismissed the bleeding as having pulled something. However, several hours later, I was using the restroom and noticed the spotting had increased. I called Scott at the hospital and asked him to see if he could get me into the obstetrician. One of the doctors performing surgery that morning was an obstetrician.

When I arrived to the OB-GYN clinic, they collected a urine sample and released me for work. They assured me that they would call with the results as soon as they received them. However, instead of hearing the results, I was asked to come back in. After checking in, they sent me to the lab for blood work and instructions to return to the clinic afterward.

Forty-five minutes later, Dr. Voss came in to see me. He told me I was pregnant, but he was concerned that I was going to have a miscarriage. He sent me home for a week of bed rest. The spotting stopped, and I returned to work. The pregnancy was complicated. I went into early labor at five months and was on bed rest for the remainder of the pregnancy. Even with the bed rest, I was hospitalized twice to stop early labor.

We were ecstatic when Corey made his entrance into the world in December 1987. He was a healthy and beautiful baby, and I began to believe that I could be happy again. He brought such joy into our lives. With each new milestone, we discovered the many blessings of being first-time parents: his first gooing sounds, holding the bottle, saying Mama and Dada, and crawling. Babies are such a blessing if we stop and take the time to enjoy and love them before it is too late.

In the summer of 1989, we received orders for a PCS to Germany. We had never been outside of Texas except as very small children, and we were so excited. It was to be a new adventure for us, and we could not wait for it to start. The only drawback occurred when we were shocked to find out that Corey could not travel with us. He would have to remain with a family member until we could acquire off-base housing. Post housing had an extremely long waiting list that awarded housing by rank and then years in service. It broke our hearts to walk down the jet way without our baby boy. The only family stable enough to leave Corey with was my parents, and that did not sit well with either of us. Finding housing became our number one priority.

It took us two very long months to find housing. However, when we did, it was an amazing place. We had a ground-level flat with a backyard for Corey to play in. Two German flight attendants lived above us who spoke English and helped us so much. As soon as the army verified our rental agreement, one of us could fly back to Houston to bring Corey home in time for his second birthday and our first Christmas in Germany.

Scott was a wonderful father and knew how hard not having Corey had been on me. He quickly suggested that I be the one to bring our baby boy home. The flight home seemed to last forever, but when I saw our baby, none of that mattered any more. The four days of getting everything ready for our return flight were slower than snails. We just wanted to be home with Scott. In no time, we settled into a routine, and we were happy again. Not even the rapes could penetrate our happy world.

Life in Germany was wonderful. On our days off, we would go adventuring or sightseeing. It is such a beautiful country. Christmas in Germany was and continues to be one of my most cherished memories. Many who travel to Germany do so during the warm months of summer, but there are special treats available for those who came during the off-season. Christmas in Germany is a magical time and there are all sorts of experiences you can have that summer tourists will miss.

Throughout the country, Christmas markets—sometimes known as Kris Kringle marts—begin opening during the last week of November. It doesn't matter where you are; in villages, towns, and cities, there is almost always at least one Kris Kringle Mart. It's in these markets that you can find some of the most authentic German goods, because they are all hand-made. Each of the stalls in a Kris Kringle Mart offers different things—from delicious baked goods, to toys, to fine leatherwork.

The history and traditions of Christmas in Germany is quite interesting. The name we often use for Santa Claus, Kris Kringle, originally evolved out of the word Christkindl, or "Christ Child." Additionally, we derive all manner of Christmas traditions from the German culture. The Adventskalender, those festive looking calendars featuring a 24 day count up to Christmas disguised as windows and doors, was originally created by the Germans. As one of the Christmas customs, candles or chocolates will be placed inside the paper windows as treats for children prior to Christmas.

Music is central to Christmas in Germany as well and a few of our more popular holiday songs originate from Germany. The most famous of these is Silent Night, having been translated into 44 different languages.

And of course no German Christmas would be complete without a tree. The tradition of decorating the tree extends far back in German history and even includes a twist. Traditionally, the Christmas customs dictate that the tree is presented assembled prior to the Christmas meal. However, children are not allowed to see the tree before then. Often times, the children will be sent off to be occupied while the parents decorate it with lights, ornaments, and cookies. Presents are placed beneath the boughs of the tree and when the time is right, the children are brought back in the room to sing carols and open gifts. The secrecy of some of the Christmas customs in Germany greatly enhances the holiday for both the children and the adults. As a result, there's little reason to wonder why Christmas is such a prominent holiday and can still bring a cherished smile when recalled.

My work was an hour and a half from Frankfurt in the small town of Rüsselsheim. I often took the tram to the train depot and then rode the train into the office. It was such a beautiful ride, and it dropped me just two blocks from the office. I loved riding the train until February 2, 1990, when a train disaster occurred directly across from an American military post on the main railway near the Rüsselsheim station. Upon hearing the collision, the entire company ran outside to see what had occurred. We saw tangled steel and metal twisted and wrapped around each other and people on the ground everywhere we looked. With seventeen persons killed and 145 severely injured, the train collision is amongst the most serious in rapid transit. I will never forget the carnage of that day.

At 16:42, the regular train of the Rhine-Main S-Bahn entered the Rüsselsheim station. The mass rapid transit DB Class 420 train was on its way from Mainz to Frankfurt on the S14 line. The station was secured with distant signals before the station platforms and stop signals after the station platforms technically enforced by Indusi inductors. The train driver acknowledged the warning of the distant signal (1000 Hz Indusi) but he had forgotten about it after dispatching the train in daily routine.

A second DB Class 420 train was oncoming from Frankfurt; however, in contrast to daily routine, another train was already on the regular platform. The train was diverted to another platform at the other side of the station, requiring the train to cross the track of the first train before the station. Both trains were fully packed during rush hour with an estimate of five hundred passengers per train.

Although the main signal was on stop a few hundred meters after the station, the driver accelerated quickly after leaving the station. The regular speed of S-Bahn trains is about eighty kilometers per hour, and the powerful trains can attain that easily. Although both trains had activated the emergency brakes—also enforced by an automated train stop (2000 Hz Indusi) on the main signal—the collision occurred at a speed estimated to be between forty and seventy kilometers per hour for both trains. The collision was so intense that one of the control cars was lifted upright into the air before falling to the side on a nearby car park.

Our lives became even more wonderful when we found out we were expecting again six months later. I loved being a mother and could not wait to welcome another baby into our lives. I could not have asked for a better father for my children. Any time the baby needed tending to, and we were both home, we shared the experience with enthusiasm and joy. We could not wait to hold the tiny baby growing inside my tummy and experience all the firsts again with our new blessing. When I breastfed the baby, Scott would change him and then rock him back to sleep. Once he was weaned and on a bottle, we would switch off feeding and changing responsibilities.

Scott loved to ride his bike to work at the hospital. Since the daycare center was next door to the hospital, he bought a child carrier so they could ride to and from work together.

Scott was the better parent on most days. I had never been an early riser and definitely did not deal well with getting up all hours of the night. It would take forever for me to get back to sleep, and Scott would be snoring within minutes. I never understood how he could do that. It still takes forever to fall back asleep if I wake up during the night or early morning.

Unfortunately, being a transportation specialist required early mornings and long hours. As an operating room technician, Scott had short hours and flexible days. He took on many of the nighttime duties.

When we had free time, we loved going bowling on Wednesdays at Rhein-Main Air Force Base. We would end our day by taking Corey to watch the planes take off and land. We also enjoyed hiking in the forest and parks in the beautiful mountains. We would take turns carrying Corey on our backs as we explored. When we hiked, we would make a day of it by packing a picnic basket, wine, and a blanket. Seldom did we leave Corey with a sitter; if we did, it was only with someone we personally knew.

Due to the complications with our first pregnancy, we decided that I would separate from the army and become a stay-at-home mother. I was so excited to be able to stay home with our baby boy and soon-to-be newborn. I had always dreamed about it, but it was not a possibility as a soldier. Once the army confirmed that I would be given a hardship separation with an honorable discharge, we began making plans and looking for a bigger flat to rent. When it came time to separate from the army, we celebrated with joy. We were starting a new chapter in our lives. Our babies would have their mommy at home to care for them instead of being taken care of by strangers at a daycare center. I looked forward to bringing our baby home.

I officially separated from the army in June 1990. I traveled back to the United States with Corey. We had decided that it would be best to finish out the final three months of the pregnancy with my family. We wanted our baby to be born in the United States instead of a foreign country. In June, Corey and I flew back to Houston. It was exciting being home, but we both missed Scott so much. At times, we wondered if we had made the right decision. We called as often as we could afford; during one of those rare calls, Scott said he had requested leave and would be with us soon.

On July 18, Scott joined us for two weeks. Scott was part of a special medical team that would deploy to South Africa for six months to host mobile medical clinics and inoculate children. He was so excited about the Africa trip, and then he would have only one more month before he came back to Texas for the birth. We would join him as soon as our newborn could fly. Feeling blessed, we could not wait for the next chapter of our life to begin.

While Scott was on leave, we scheduled an appointment with my doctor. We were so excited to meet the doctor who was going to deliver our baby. To us, it was a perfect appointment; we listened to the heartbeat and stared in awe at the tiny being on the ultrasound monitor. It was so amazing that such a tiny thing could make us so giggly. The doctor informed us that we would finally find out if we would be blessed with another baby boy or a baby girl at the next week's appointment. As soon as we left the doctor's office, we begin picking out names for a boy and a girl. After much debate, and a little arguing, we chose Dakota Garrett for a boy and Ashley Nichole for a girl. We both wanted a baby girl more than anything in the world.

We spent the week window-shopping and deciding what the baby's room would look like, depending on the sex. We took Corey to the park and watched him run around and play as we talked.

Scott laughingly said, "This time next year, you will be chasing after two little ones."

Although it had only been a month since we had left Germany, it seemed like years had passed. We did not know who missed the other more. At night, Scott would rub my tummy and talk to the baby before turning Bach on. He believed that playing music to them would increase their learning once born. As silly as it seemed then, I am inclined to agree with him now. We did that with all three kids, and they are all extremely intelligent.

Even with so much going on, the week dragged by as we waited for our next appointment. To fill the time, we went car shopping. Three days before the appointment, we found a new car. We needed a second car because we had left our car in Germany for Scott.

After several hours in the sun, I was not feeling well. After choosing the car I wanted, I asked Scott to take me back to my parents' house. In the morning, he went to fill out the loan paperwork and pick up the car. When he came home with a motorcycle, I wanted to knock him upside his head. What was he thinking? A motorcycle, really? To say I was pissed beyond pissed would not even be close to what I was feeling. As angry as I was with him, he was able to rationalize it. He often did that, made things sound so reasonable that he frequently got what he wanted. He would ship the car back, and the motorcycle was going to be shipped to Germany. It would be cheaper for gas, a smaller note, and we would save money. Finally, I gave in—even though he had never ridden a street bike. He was happy, and that was what was important.

We called Carlee and arranged for her husband to come over the next morning. Charles was going to follow Scott to the Department of Public Safety to take his motorcycle-driving exam. As we talked in bed that night, we were so excited about our future. We had overcome so much, and life was finally looking up for us. We talked about the appointment, how we would finally find out if we were having a boy or a girl, and his motorcycle test. He was confident and assured me that everything would be all right.

When we woke up, he was like a kid in a toy store. During breakfast with my parents, we talked about the names we had chosen and Scott's deployment to Africa. He felt honored to be on the team. He considered it a privilege and a once-in-a-lifetime learning experience.

As the morning passed, Scott was getting anxious and wanted to leave early. Telling him to be patient was a waste of time and breath, and assuring him that Carlee and Charles would arrive soon was not working. Neither did reminding him that the appointment was not until

3:30. At 2:55, he decided he was going to leave. He asked Charles to meet him at the DMV. Sure enough, within seconds of Scott leaving, they pulled in. Carlee got out, and Charles went to meet Scott.

At 2:59 on July 24, a drunk driver ran a red light and turned right in front of him. He tried to lay the motorcycle down, but he did not make it in time. He hit the front right fender, and the impact broke his neck. His life was cut way too short at twenty-two, and our world was turned upside down.

He did all the right things. He wore a helmet and did as he had learned when he was riding dirt bikes as a kid. He tried to lay down the bike to lessen the impact. However, none of that saved him. Charles was two cars behind Scott when the accident happened. Within a minute, he approached the accident scene to see if he could help. When he saw Scott in the road, he went into shock. It took the police officers and EMS technicians a little over an hour to get him calm enough to call us.

When I answered the phone, Charles asked to speak to Carlee. I knew instantly that something was terribly wrong. As Scott left, we were going through some boxes in the garage, and I had a sudden intake of breath. It was like being punched in the stomach. Mom and

Carlee worried it was labor and sent me in to lie down. Therefore, when Charles called, something in me already knew Scott was dead. I said, "Just tell me. I already know he is dead. Just tell me."

He kept asking to speak to Carlee, but I knew in my heart that Scott was dead. I cannot explain how, but I knew it as sure as I was breathing. I called Carlee to the phone, and her face confirmed what I had already known. We began to scream and cry as we collapsed in disbelief and devastation. How could it be true when he had just left? How? Why?

Carlee wanted to go to the accident site to be with her husband, and I demanded to go as well. To this day, I wish we had never gone there. For years, I have attempted to erase that image, but I never really have. The image of our two-and-a-half-year-old son begging his daddy to wake up will forever be ingrained in my memory. He looked like he was just sleeping.

I fainted and woke up in an ambulance. They were worried about the stress causing a miscarriage. I am so thankful to say that my baby was strong, and we had no complications.

Our lives changed forever in just a matter of minutes. All of our hopes and dreams for our children and our marriage had been ripped right out of our hands. In the passing of a moment, my husband was gone forever. I was a single mother of a two-and-a-half-year-old and was six months pregnant. Our children would never have the opportunity to know their father; much less experience his unconditional love.

As they grew up, I tried to reassure them that their daddy loved them very much, but I do not think it ever really made a difference to them. They did not have a father, and that was all that mattered to them. He was not there to tuck them in at night, hold them when they cried, watch them play sports, or hear about their first dates. There was a hole in their hearts that could not be filled—not even by me.

After that life-altering phone call, we faced planning a funeral. Who has made their death wishes known at twenty-three—and much less planned a funeral? In a moment's notice, we were choosing coffins, music, bible verses, burial location, and food for the viewing. There were so many decisions to make without any advanced planning. It felt like a drunken haze; everything swirled around. I was not sure if it was really happening.

On the day of the funeral, I wanted to die with him, but I knew my kids needed me. *How could this be happening to us?* We dressed and waited for the limo. Most people do not even ride in a limo when they are alive, but they ride in them for a funeral. His funeral was like a movie in slow motion, yet there was so much that had been lost.

The chapel was full that day. People sometimes say they have not seen me since the funeral, but I can only remember a handful of them. I do recall the military trumpet bellowing out that lonesome melody, the twenty-one-gun salute, or the soldiers folding the flag. However, I do remember, the soldier who handed me Scott's flag had the surname Stewart. How ironic, we were burying our Stewart.

My separation from the army had only been a month prior to Scott's death; therefore, I had no job or income. Everything we owned—our furniture, car, and even our bank accounts—were in Germany. I often wonder how I survived that first year after his death. The one blessing that I do remember was being told that I was having a girl. On November 10, 1990, I went into labor and brought the most beautiful baby girl I have ever seen into this crazy world. I blessed her with the name her father and I had so carefully and lovingly chosen for her. Our angel could not have been any more perfect.

We sat through the trial of the man who tore our world apart. We watched in anger and astonishment as he laughed and joked with his family and attorney. I tried to soothe two heartbroken babies.

After his death, I guarded my two babies like prisoners. They did not stay with anyone but my sister or me. Always terrified they would be taken away as well; I cursed God and turned away from him and my faith. I did not understand how a loving God could allow this to happen to such a good man. What was wrong with God? Why would he allow something so terrible to happen to me again? Weren't my childhood or the rapes enough? So many thoughts and doubts plagued me during those first few dark lonely years after his death.

I closed myself off and closed my feelings off so I would never be hurt again. I was numb to life and love. I became an empty shell, just walking through life without living it or enjoying it. I loved my babies, but I could not show it with the tender hugs and kisses that children should be showered with. I took care of them, fed them, and made sure they had clean clothes, but I never fully opened my heart and arms to them.

The fear of my babies being taken away consumed my thoughts, which led me to completely shut my emotions off. I thought that if I loved them or showed my love for them, something bad was surely going to happen to them. I lived in constant fear and wondered if today would be the day. Which one of them will be taken from me? In my mind, I knew that they would be taken from me.

They are now adults, but when the phone rings with an unknown number, I am too terrified to answer it because the fear of losing one of them still overwhelms me. The fear has also affected the quality of life for my family. I thought nothing bad would happen to them if I could control everything they did, where they went, and who they hung out with. This behavior, which has carried over into their adult lives, has caused many conflicts. Our relationships have come close to being severed.

During the last six months of therapy, I have realized that controlling them is not a healthy behavior for any of us. However, the behavior did not develop overnight and cannot be changed overnight. It is a daily inner battle that is won some days and lost on other days.

Learning that it is helpful and healing to share the symptoms of PTSD with the family has helped our relationships tremendously. There is more work needed, but instead of hopelessness and control, my actions are now led by love. There are years of hurt and pain that must be undone, but I am confident that with continued treatment and by actively using the skills I've learned, those scars will fade until they are replaced with love, laughter, and many wonderful memories. There is no longer hopelessness in my life, only hopefulness for the future.

Life went on even though we thought it could not without Scott. Corey begun to have nightmares and would wake up in the middle of the night crying for his daddy. He went from being a vivacious, carefree little boy to a clingy needy little boy. If I left a room, he was right behind or beside me. He even had to be with me when I was taking a shower. He would sit on the rug beside the shower and talk to me the entire time. It became so bad that his pediatrician advised therapy. After several sessions, they diagnosed him with separation anxiety and told me to just be patient. With time, he returned to the loving outgoing little boy.

We missed Scott so very much, and at times, we were convinced he was still alive and would walk through the doors any day. Once while waiting in line at the bank, I stared at the man at the cashier's counter with my heart pounding. From the back, he looked just like Scott. He had the same color hair, a similar haircut, the same athletic build, and even the same height. When he turned to leave and I realized it was not Scott, my heart was broken all over.

At one point, I convinced myself that his death was staged by the military, and he was just gone on some covert mission. However, three years after his death, I accepted that he was not coming home to us. As much as we loved and missed him, life had to continue. With two babies to raise on my own, my time for mourning was long over. The children needed me to be there for them; however, unknown to me, I had already withdrawn many emotions and built up walls. Being a single parent is hard enough on its own, but when you add the death of one of the parents, raising the kids is even more difficult. There were no weekend breaks while at Dad's, no help with child support, no sharing holidays, and no help with discipline—it was *all* on me. I had to do everything as well as—if not better than—a dual-parent household. It became a vicious cycle that was doomed for failure.

Eventually, out of loneliness and fear of dying alone, I begin to date again. One evening, a friend convinced me to go dancing. I met a charming man and began to look forward to life again. He was a divorcee with two daughters who lived in Tennessee with their mother. He was living with his parents because he had recently packed up and moved back to Texas.

After dating for a couple of months, he talked me into letting him move in with us. Within a few months, I became pregnant with my third child. Knowing I was not in love with John, I convinced myself that it was better than being alone. For the sake of our beautiful unborn son, I tried to make it work, but John was an alcoholic who would not—or could not—keep a job or stay sober. He preferred to play video games and drink a twelve pack or more every day.

In December 1993, Joseph was born. He was such a beautiful little boy. I felt so blessed to have my three angelic babies. By the time Joseph was born, John and I were sleeping in separate rooms. I just could not bring myself to kick him out since there were two kids that had to be raised without a father already. Corey was six, Nichole was three, and they loved having a baby brother. Life went on, and we adapted to the changes. Corey started playing T-ball and flag football, and Nichole was a cheerleader for whatever activity he was involved in at the time. When she was old enough, she began ballet lessons and loved it. They were growing up so fast.

In October of 1994, after working as the commander at the American Legion post, I crawled into my bed. Everyone was already asleep, including Joseph. When we got up the next morning, I needed to run some errands. I rushed around to get everything straightened up before leaving to run the errands.

After finishing the dishes, I ran some bath water and undressed Joseph. I was shocked and angry to see bruises in the shape of a fingerprints running up and down his little thigh. After bathing and quickly dressing, I got Joseph ready. We went straight to Corey and Nichole's school and signed them out.

Once we were all in the car, I asked them about the bruises on Joseph's leg. They said Joseph had fallen down, bumped his head, and started crying. When John came into the living room to see what had happened, he started yelling at Joseph to stop crying. Nichole said Joseph would not stop crying, and John slapped him on his leg and said, "Now you have a reason to cry."

Corey finished the story. He explained how John continued to yell at him to stop crying. When he did not, John would hit him on his leg again.

As soon as they finished, I drove straight to an attorney's office. The kids explained how Joseph had gotten the bruises. Upon hearing the kids' accounts, the attorney photographed the bruises to save for future evidence. He advised me that I did not have to file for a divorce since we had never married, I did not use his last name, and we did not file taxes together. However, he would keep a file with the pictures in case there was ever a need for them in the future.

After thanking him, we went home. I got the kids a snack and settled them down with a movie. I placed everything that belonged to John into trash bags and set them out by the curb. I called him and told him that his belongings were by the curb—and if he even set one toe on my property, he would be shot. We never saw him get his belongings, but they were gone the next morning.

Once John was out of our lives, the kids and I were happier than we had been in a while. I had found a job at the high school and started going to college. I was determined to finish the degree I had started working on in 1986 as a private in the army. Life was looking up, and the kids were happy.

Two months later, our happy world was shattered by a knock on the door. When I answered it, John pushed his way into the house and screamed that he was going to take Joseph with him. I tried to push him back out the door and yelled for Corey to call 911. I could smell the alcohol on his breath as I was yelling at him to get out of my house.

Corey came running up to me with the phone because the dispatcher needed my address. While I was trying to give it to her,

John tried to grab Joseph again. Out of natural instinct, I swung my arm toward him, trying to prevent him from getting a hold of Joseph. The phone struck him right below his eye and caught him off guard. He let go of Joseph and took a step back. I shoved him out the door and locked it. I yelled for Corey to take his brother and sister into my bathroom, lock the door, and not come out until I came for them.

When the officers arrived, John was still banging on the door and screaming and cussing. As the two officers approached the house, I opened the front door and stepped out onto the porch. The older officer asked what was going on. As I started to explain, John cut me off and started yelling about me not letting him see his son. Not long into John's tirade, the younger officer said he would interview John, and the other one motioned me into the house. I gave my side of the incident, and the officer asked me to have the kids come out so he could talk them since they had seen and heard everything.

I did not like the idea of the kids being questioned since they had already been traumatized enough. I tried explaining this to the police officer and told him that Corey was only eight, Nichole was five, and Joseph was shy of his second birthday. I expressed that I was not sure talking to them was a good idea, but I eventually gave in. I called for Corey to bring Nichole and Joseph so the officer could talk to them.

The officer ended up only talking to Corey. After doing so, he went out to speak with his partner. However, before he made it outside, the officer who was interviewing John came in and asked if I would allow John to hold the baby while he finished speaking to him. Since the officers were there, I saw no harm in it and handed Joseph over to the officer. Both officers walked outside to talk. When they reached John, the officer with Joseph stopped and handed him to John. After fifteen minutes, I went to the porch and asked for Joseph.

John said, "No. You are not getting him back."

We began to argue again. The officers came back to where we were standing, and the officer who had interviewed me told me to get Joseph's diaper bag ready for John. I told him I was not giving him Joseph's bag because Joseph was not leaving with him.

I was dumfounded when he explained that Texas law said whoever had physical custody (who was physically holding him) of the child, is who they had to leave that child with since there was no court-ordered custody agreement. They totally overlooked the fact that John reeked of alcohol. To add insult to injury, they said I could not file breaking and entering charges. Since I had not had him evicted through the courts, it was still his home—and he could come and go as he pleased. I was floored. I could not believe what was happening!

I argued with the officers, and the threat of being arrested for interfering with their duty and domestic violence, made me get the diaper bag. The other kids still needed their mommy. When I approached the front door with the diaper bag, I overheard an officer say, "I am married to a bitch as well. We are going through a nasty divorce. So any time I can help a man out, I do."

I was in my attorney's office the next day, but even with a court order, it took three months to get Joseph back home with us. That was the longest three months of our lives. Corey and Nichole did not understand why their little brother was not with us—and neither did I. John would not let us see or talk to Joseph during those long torturous months. I later learned that he and Joseph had been staying at his girlfriend's house so that we could not find them. The courts and law enforcement could not seem to locate John to serve him with the custody papers—if they were ever even looking for him. My father contacted John's parents, and he told them that John had until six o'clock that evening to have Joseph back to me per the custody agreement. If not, he would not live to ever do this again. Joseph was home with us by six o'clock that night, and all was right in our lives again. However, the control and fear of impending doom increased tenfold. People were not invited or allowed into our lives, and on the rare occasion someone was, they were watched with a hawk's eye and never completely trusted.

We were so happy to be back together again, but the battle with John never ended. Joseph is almost twenty years old, and his father still owes around $28,000 in unpaid child support. He said that he was not going to support me, but he would get Joseph what he needed when he was with him. Looking back on it now, I wish I had taken him to court, but I ended up procrastinating until it was too late.

My guilt about Corey and Nichole not having a father influenced my decisions to our detriment. There were times we survived on very little food, went without electricity for up to a week until payday, or had the water shut off. Before I kicked him out, we bought two new cars, both financed in my name. I kept one, and he took the other. Since the payments were more than I could afford, I sold our car and bought an older, cheaper car for cash. When the transmission went out eight months later, I tried to finance another car. I found out that the car John had been driving had been repossessed for nonpayment. Several credit cards I knew nothing about had been reported in default as well.

Those experiences only reinforced my lack of trust and faith in people and caused me to close down emotionally once again. Allowing no one into our life, I became even more controlling over my children. I did not allow them to go to very many people's homes because I had no faith that they would be okay without me. My oldest son was only allowed to spend nights with his best friend. Nichole only stayed with my sister or my parents. Against my better judgment, Joseph would stay with his father on visitation days as ordered by the courts.

The kids became my entire world, but as I look back on it now, it was not a healthy behavior for them or me. Distrust consumed me and fueled my isolation from other adults. I did not socialize or make friends because I no longer had trust in the human race. I spent my time at my kids' activities, going to college, and working. The only thing that was important was raising my babies and ensuring their safety.

That behavior caused me to lose myself as a parent. I felt so guilty about Scott's death and for Joseph not having his father in his life (besides every other weekend). Because of the guilt, I stopped parenting and became their friend. I was always trying to prove that one parent was enough. I gave them everything they wanted—even when I could not afford it. Sometimes I overdrew my accounts to get things without regard of the consequences. Before long, more was going out than was coming in, and we had to sell the home I had bought after Scott's death because I could not pay the taxes.

In 1997, we moved to Livingston and rented a house near my parents. Mom used her connections to help me get hired as a jailer with our local sheriff's department. Because she had worked in some aspect of law enforcement most of our childhood, I was familiar with the position and was excited about starting. Being a jailer involved of a lot, but I still loved the job. In fact, several months into the job, some co-workers were discussing the police academy. I was not one to listen in on other people's conversations, but the conversation held my full attention. One of my childhood dreams had been to be a police officer. I applied to the law enforcement academy along with them.

I was accepted to the academy and was soon learning the responsibilities of being a Texas peace officer. I learned the Texas penal code, report writing, arrest procedures, criminal investigations, self-defense techniques, firearms training, crime scene investigation, traffic enforcement and investigations, patrol tactics, emergency vehicle operation, physical fitness training, firearms training, and standardized field sobriety testing. After months of rigorous training, our class graduated as peace officers in October 1997.

After graduating the academy, I became a reserve police officer in Jasper, a rural town, and trained under Sergeant Cain. Being in the field was a lot different from what I learned in the classroom. Sergeant Cain rode in the patrol car while we were serving warrants. As were driving through town, he spotted one of the individuals we had a warrant on walking down the side of the road. As soon as he saw the patrol car, he took off running Sergeant. Cain hit the ditch, while throwing the car in park, while I jumped out all in one smooth motion.

I'm not sure how long or how far we ran through the woods and briar patches, but I eventually called it quits and worked my way back toward the patrol car. I'm not sure where Sergeant Cain had gone, but I kept thinking I would meet up with him at some point. He was sitting in the air-conditioned car smiling. Hot, sweaty, and covered in briars, I asked him why he did not back me up.

Chuckling he said, "Why would I? We know who he is and where he lives."

Pissed and a little embarrassed, I said, "Then why he let me chase him?"

Chuckling again, he said, "As your training officer, it is my job to train you. Did you learn something?"

Under his guidance, many valuable lessons were taught and learned. From there, I worked as an undercover narcotics police officer for one of the local towns. I did not want to do that kind of work in the same town I lived in because of the risk of retaliation. The adrenaline rush was addictive; the more I did it, the more I wanted to do it again. Playing the part of a drug addict trying to score while using a confidential informant to make the contact with a drug dealer was dangerous and thrilling. No two days were ever the same. Nevertheless, in a small rural town, I could only do it for so long before being burned. This was referred to as "being made."

When possible, I worked on achieving my dream of completing the degree I'd started eleven years earlier. With the risk my career involved, I became even more obsessed with keeping my kids safe. I inserted myself even more into everything they participated in. If they played it, I became their T-ball, flag football, cheer, and dance mom. I was room mother for all three of my children's classrooms and attended as many class trips as possible. Whatever they were active in, I was right there with them. No one could keep them safer than their own mom could—or that is what I had convinced myself of.

Even when taking college classes, I would drag my books with me to watch them practice or participate in a game and try to do my homework at the same time. For eight years after the disaster of the relationship with John, the kids were all that I needed to be happy—or so I thought.

Working as an undercover officer was hectic and demanding, and I was excited about finally having a weekend off. The kids and I had plans for a visit with my sister, and we headed to Houston after I picked them up early from school. The kids settled into playing outside, and my sister told me that a friend had invited us to go to the Houston Livestock Show and Rodeo. Since they had an extra ticket, she asked them if I could go too.

It had been such a long time since going out that my habit was to say no thank you. I tried to beg off by telling her that the kids were there, but she quickly shot that excuse down. She had already arranged with her husband keep the kids, and there was no reason we could not go. Reluctantly I agreed to go, and as the day wore on, I realized that I was actually looking forward to some adult time with my sister. It dawned on me that I had not allowed personal happiness into my life in a long time.

Carlee backed out at the last minute because one of her twins had a fever, and she was worried that four kids and one of them being sick was more that Charles could handle. Her friends extended the invitation to go along with them anyway, and I grudgingly agreed. When they asked if I wanted to ride with them or drive, already planning an exit strategy, I said I would follow them. After we arrived and parked, we met up with some of their friends. They made introductions, and surprisingly, I felt as if I had known several of them for years. Looking back, we had more in common than they knew since they were police officers as well. As cops, they were already well on their way celebrating. There was a bonfire and several barbecue pits with briskets, links, and ribs—and an endless supply of beer and liquor. I had never acquired a taste for beer or liquor, and when they asked what kind of drink I wanted, I did not know what to ask for. Char, the woman who invited me, suggested milk punch. It went down smooth with only a small hint of liquor, and I managed to relax enough that I was enjoying myself.

Later that evening, I was actually having a great time. As the night wore on—and after a couple of drinks—I began to open up and talk to some of the people. However, when asked what I did for a living, I lied and said I was a teacher. I still don't know why I said that! I had taught the kids to say if they were asked.

Char and I lost touch after several months. However, two people from that night have had a lasting impact on me. J. K. was a police officer for the Houston Police Department and became a very dear friend. Months or years could pass, but when we talked, it was as if we had just talked the day before—and that is still true today.

Something was about to happen that would change our lives forever. It was getting late and cold. With as much fun as it was, I wanted to get back to my babies. However, Char wanted me to stay to meet a friend. He was a marine who was right down the road at the Marine Reserve center. He was conducting weekend drills and would be arriving at any minute. I did not want to stay—and I certainly did not want to meet anyone—but I felt obligated because Char had issued the invitation to the rodeo.

Thank God I stayed that night and waited to meet the marine. I will never forget the moment Charles stepped out of his truck in his military fatigues. I fell in love on the spot and knew that someday soon I was going to marry him. He instantly brought to the surface emotions and feelings that I had long since buried. I did not believe that I would ever be in love again.

When Char introduced us, I remember thinking that he had the most beautiful blue eyes. Actually, at times, they were blue, and at other times, they appeared grey. He was so outgoing and friendly. It seemed as if he knew everyone, and his laugh was contagious and affected everyone else. The three of us walked over to stand by the bonfire in an attempt to fight off the cold while David headed off to make Charles a drink. Charles made small talk with several of the cops around us while Char quizzed me about what I thought of him. Eventually, we migrated beside each other, and before we knew it, we had talked the night away.

I invited Charles to the rodeo again the next night, and he accepted. He said we would have hook up there after he was finished with his drills. I was elated when he agreed, and exhilarating and terrifying feelings and emotions overwhelmed me. Not wanting the night to end, but knowing that it had too, we exchanged numbers and said goodnight.

The next day, Charles called to say his drill was going to run later than expected. After two days of drills, he was dragging. He asked if we could have dinner at his home and even offered to cook. Of course, I accepted. We talked for a few more minutes, and he ended the call by saying that he would pick up a movie on his way home. Just hearing his voice had butterflies fluttering around in my tummy—not to mention other long-forgotten sensations. He still has that effect fifteen years later.

As the day wore on, panic and doubt bombarded me; after all, he was virtually a stranger. What did it matter if he was a marine; they can be serial killers too. The closer it came time for me to leave, the more fear and anxiety wreaked havoc on my. I was scared of being hurt and terrified about agreeing to go to his house. I cannot recall how many times I picked up the phone to cancel our date. However, before it could even ring, I would hang it up.

An hour before our date, Char called to see if we were still having dinner—and to reaffirm that he was a great person. Before she realized it, she had agreed to drive. If I felt comfortable being alone with Charles, she would come back and pick me up. Otherwise, I do not believe I would have kept our date.

When I arrived with Char in tow, Charles took it in stride. He poured us drinks, and we talked as he prepared dinner. He grilled steaks with sautéed mushrooms and onions and a stuffed baked potato as we sipped wine and talked. We were having a great time, and Charles invited Char to stay and watch the movie with us. The three of us were like best friends; we talked and laughed without any effort or odd silences. Being able to relax and enjoy spending time with other people felt great. While sitting with them, I realized just how much I had missed that feeling.

The steak was one of the best I had ever eaten. It was so tender, and the flavoring was delicious. It was the first time I'd eaten a steak without steak sauce; it certainly did not require one. His culinary skills were very impressive. As we ate, drank wine, and talked, we realized that we had talked the night away again. We still do that after so many years.

Charles is currently a contractor in Afghanistan, and we spend three to four hours a night talking. That night, we were so involved in talking and getting to know each other that we did not notice that Char had fallen asleep during the movie. Once we began talking, we could not tell anyone what the movie was about—even if our lives depended on it. Charles had drills on Sunday morning and had to be up in four hours. We pulled out the hide-a-bed for Char and me. When we left at six, we had a date for that night. We have been together since that weekend.

A year later, we moved in together. Charles accepted the role of being a father to the three kids, and we accepted his son into our lives. My kids were looking forward to having an older brother.

Unfortunately, they never really were able to know Gordon since he lived hours away in Corpus Christi with his mom and stepdad. We did not get to see him nearly as often as we would have liked. Charles was busy with the marine reserves and his job with the Drug Enforcement Administration. Gordon earned his Eagle Scout Badge in Boy Scouts and was on the swim team.

Now that Gordon is grown and Charles has retired, they are making up for lost time. Gordon graduated from college and is a firefighter in Arizona. The kids still are not as close as we would like them to be, but when they leave home and start their own lives, it became more difficult than it already was. We have not given up on the hope that they will all be close someday and realize how important it is to have a strong family bond.

To say life with me was not easy would be an oxymoron. I still hold onto the old fears, the pain of being raped, and all the emotional and mental scars. They were like landmines waiting to implode. As much as I tried to suppress the memories and nightmares, they seemed to always be there. I was plagued by them during the day and chased by them by night.

It was ruining the quality of life for all of us, especially those who were closest to me. For as much as Charles and I loved each other, I could not bring myself to completely trust him. There were two reasons behind this lack of trust. I did not trust men in general, and I had abandonment issues. If Scott could walk out the door for something as mundane as getting a driver's licenses and never come back to me, then Charles could too. Even though Scott had no say in that drunk driver taking his life, it still left a feeling abandonment. I was extremely controlling with Charles; it was as if he was one of the kids.

I lived in fear that Charles would walk out the door one day and not come back. Fear had controlled me daily; I was afraid of his plane crashing or someone killing him in the line of duty. These thoughts engulfed me completely and made me hold on even more tightly. The fear, consumed every waking moment; in my mind, I just knew something bad was going to happen to the kids or to Charles or to all of them. I was so consumed by fear of being abandoned that it never dawned on me that I was pushing them out of my life through my irrational thinking and behavior.

If Charles did not call when he said, I always overreacted. I would work myself into a panic attack, which often led to a complete meltdown. I threatened to leave him because if I left first, he would not be able to leave and hurt me. I just knew he was going to leave. I would call his pager, cell phone, and office line until I reached him, which led to many arguments between us. It also caused tension and turmoil with his co-workers. With time, I have come to understand that no one knew of the battle within me because it showed weakness—and I would never be weak again. They only saw the craziness of my actions.

My control over the kids became even more drastic as did the detachment from everything. I was numb to life because if I did not feel anything, I could not be hurt. I was convinced by this belief, and my actions soon mirrored my thoughts. If something happened to any of them, it would not hurt me.

Looking back now, I believe that this detachment kept us together. Charles had been abandoned during his first marriage. He was detached too. Although we were together, by not being 100 percent committed, we could never be hurt again. Looking back, it is clear to see how our lack of emotional attachment hurt the kids. Our kids lived in a home in which all of their materialistic needs and wants were provided for; however, all they ever really wanted was to feel loved and accepted.

It was as if we were there but never *totally* there. The harder we tried to be happy, the more out of control our life became. Even with the love and security that should have come with our marriage, the nightmares were still inside my head. They became even more graphic.

I was in a constant state of fear, dreading and waiting for something bad to happen. It drained the life out of me—mentally, physically, and emotionally. Life passed by, and I continued to struggle with trust, my temper, irrational behavior, depression, and uncontrollable spending. *Why must the happiness everyone seems to enjoy elude me? What is wrong? What have I done to deserve this? Why am I being punished?*

The symptoms increased tenfold—from walking around with a chip on my shoulder trying to prove to the world I was not a victim to jumping and startling at the slightest things. I was a nervous wreck. If Charles or the kids walked up without warning, even just for a hug, I would freak out. If he came home late from work and got into bed without advanced warning, I would wake up screaming and fighting him.

Even the innocence of thunderstorms was terrifying because the first time I was raped by First Sergeant Higgans, I could hear the thunder and see the lightning as it lit up the small window in that dark room. During a thunderstorm, the nightmares became so lifelike that I slept with a gun on Charles's pillow when he was not home. When it was not on his pillow, my faithful companion was loaded, locked, and ready to go on the nightstand.

Charles and the kids knew they had better give advance warning before opening the bedroom door. The kids could be in the house and would have to call to say they were coming in the room, especially if I was already in bed for the night. Regardless of the time, Charles would call right as he was pulling into our driveway because they all lived with the fear of accidently startling me and being shot.

Life in a Daze

Life spirals out of control

As I struggle for a tiny hold.

Wondering if I will ever reach the end of this maze,

Days slip into nights and nights into days.

Peace and joy elude me,

I just want to be free

Of living in a daze.

Charles was a devoted, loving husband, and the kids had been my world since they took their first tiny breaths, but the empty feeling would not leave. In fact, it was getting worse. I tried to fill the void with shopping, but I felt guilty for spending money beyond my earnings. It became a vicious cycle that is still a battle.

I longed to be happy like everyone else, and I did not understand why it continued to circumvent us. By that point, I was not even sure what being happy or normal even meant. As the kids got older, the symptoms worsened. Surrendering seemed to be the only option.

I am finally able to understand that they suffered as much or more as a result of my post-traumatic stress disorder. I will wear this scar until my death because I was a victim of depression!

I was rushing around to get dinner finished before Charles arrived home, and the kids would not do as they were told. They were chasing each other, and I grabbed a belt and started spanking them, while screaming and cussing. When Charles walked in, I was a shadow of my father, screaming and cussing at the kids.

He stopped dead in his tracks and said, "That is enough. They can hear you without you screaming and cussing at them."

It was as if he had knocked me upside the head. His words had the most profound impact because I had not realized what I was doing. I was doing to them what had been done to me. How had I become what I had always sworn I would never be? I never wanted my children to know the fear I had grown up with, but I was doing it to them.

That was all we had known growing up, and I was doing the same thing to my children because I had not known another way. From that day on, I made a conscious effort to change how I spoke to and disciplined my children. However, it was hard to control something when I do not know what was making me behave that way.

Post-traumatic stress disorder affected my perception of everyone else, especially my kids. Charles and I constantly accused the kids of lying, and nothing they did was ever good enough for us. We were quick to tell them how they should have done something instead of acknowledging what they had achieved. We believed we were doing our best and thought they were lucky to have parents who loved them and did as much for them as we did. Now we realize how very wrong we were. No one could have lived up to the expectations we placed on them. We expected them to be perfect—for our own reasons. I convinced myself that if they were perfect, no one would want to harm them.

At work, I was always striving to be an example of perfection, especially around male co-workers. If I was better than they were, they could not hurt or belittle me. I would push myself to the point of exhaustion and still keep going because I had to be in control! I now believe this control issue was why I went from the military into law enforcement. In that job, I felt in control.

I loved being a police officer and the prestige that came along with it; however, after a year of working as an undercover narcotics officer, I transferred to domestic violence and sex crimes. I wanted to give something back to the victims. It was important for them to have someone fighting for them. It was the one thing I never had.

Being an undercover narcotics officer gave me a false sense of power and control. My false sense of security was ripped away during a drug deal that went wrong. The confidential informer—a person we had arrested a couple of days earlier on drug charges—was offered a lesser charge if he set up a drug deal with his dealer.

The car and the informer were wired with audio and video equipment to record the entire transaction. However, he had to convince his contact to make a drug deal with an undercover officer.

The money and drugs had to through my hands during the drug deal to be legal.

We had just finished our last buy/bust for the day. A buy/bust is when we bought the drugs while the backup team was watching. Once we left the area, they went in and busted the dealer. We had just stopped at the stop sign to leave the neighborhood when a man jumped into the backseat and held a gun to my head. He screamed at me to drive. He had watched us buying drugs and was going to rob us. Thank God my lieutenant was following me and saw the man jump into my car. He called for backup. When I realized this person was going to kill me before he would surrender to arrest, I swerved the car into a sign. He was still dazed when he was taken into custody, but it was time for a change.

I loved working the domestic violence and sex crimes—until a call had a profound effect upon my life and career. I had just gone to bed when a call came in. A naked woman had run into a home while screaming for help. Hanging on the closet door, my uniform and duty belt were always ready. When late calls demanded my presence, Charles would get up and make a pot of coffee. He'd have a mug ready to go since he knew I was going to need it. While driving the thirty miles to the scene, I speculated about what I would find. However, in a million years, I could not have imagined something as horrific as what I encountered that night. The hell I had endured seemed petty compared to this.

This woman's day had started just as any other. She dropped her son off at school and went to work. Her co-workers reported that she had gone out to her car on her break and never returned. They reported their concerns to the shift supervisor. They watched the security tapes and saw a man force her into a car. They reported the kidnapping. Her nightmare had become reality; her ex-husband had kidnapped her.

For the next two days, she was brutally tortured. He drove more than two hundred miles to his parents' cabin, including an overnight stay in a hotel. He asked her questions, and if she did not respond the way he wanted, he would use a pair of pliers to pinch and twist parts of her skin off. The skin on the sides of her nose was gone; chunks from her arms, legs, thighs, and breast were gone as well. She looked as if she had survived a landmine.

Upon arriving at his parent's summer home, he chained her to a bed and continued the questioning and torture. The pliers were not enough for him; he added electrical shocks by cutting the power cord off a lamp and exposing the wiring. He kept the cord plugged in and shocked her when she said something he did not believe or agree with. She had burn marks all over her body. It was the worst domestic violence I had seen or dealt with.

On her third day in captivity, she realized she was going to have to lie if she wanted to survive this ordeal. She decided to convince him that she was being sincere and still loved him. She started confessing her love for him and said she was sorry she had left. She told him that she regretted filing for divorce and would marry him again. She begged him to be a family again, and eventually he started believing her. Sensing the change, she talked about their first date and the Chinese food they'd had, which was her favorite food. She told him that she still carried the fortune cookie in her wallet.

She had not eaten for almost two days, but she convinced him to get them the same Chinese meal they had eaten on that first date. She convinced him that they could recreate their first date and start their lives over. When he agreed to go pick up some food, he tied her up, still bloody, bruised, and naked. Using the same cord, he bound her wrist and ankles to the bedpost and went to get the food so they could re-enact their romantic first date. It would be a new beginning for them; they would be a family again.

As soon as she heard the car driving down the gravel road, she started working to free her wrist. Knowing she was working on borrowed time, she continued to struggle until she was able to free her hands and untie her ankles. As soon as she was free, she ran out of the house and searched for help. From a previous visit, she thought she remembered a house up the road. She ran toward it as fast as her shaking legs could carry her.

When she reached the house, she started screaming and banging on the door with all her might. She prayed that someone was home. Opening the door cautiously, the terrified homeowners could not believe what they were seeing. The bloody, bruised, terrified woman managed to squeeze through the small opening in the door and ran to the rear of the house while screaming and crying for help. The homeowners could not believe their eyes; they were horrified and in shock. The man hurriedly called 911, and his wife went to help the woman. She begged the homeowner to hide her. She told the frightened woman that her ex-husband had kidnapped her. She explained that if he found her, he would kill her. She was so terrified that she wedged herself into the small space between the hot water heater and the wall and refused to move.

Every cop from our rural town was there, which meant it was serious. After checking in with the officer logging in everyone at the scene, I followed the sounds of fellow officers down to the basement. She was still wedged between the wall and the hot water heater. She was still naked, bloody, and terrified.

The male officers had to leave the room because every time they approached her, she became uncontrollably hysterical. That solved one of my questions about why they were all standing around when I arrived. It took some time and reassurance to coax her out. She only came out when we had him in custody. To this day, I still think about the terror she experienced. It still amazes me how she managed to squeeze herself into that tiny space.

When she told us that he had gone out for Chinese food and would be returning to the cabin any moment, the officers set up in tactical positions and waited to take him down. There were officers waiting inside the cabin, in the woods, and farther up the road. As soon as the advanced tactical team had a visual on the suspect's car, they radioed the command sergeant. He updated the tactical team, and they took the man into custody without incident.

One of our officers had promised her proof that we had him in custody. True to his word, a Polaroid was delivered that showed the man on the ground in cuffs with three officers holding him down. After seeing the photo, she agreed to come out in order for the emergency medical technicians to stabilize and transport her to the hospital.

She flipped out when the two male emergency medical technicians approached us. It took another hour for two female emergency medical technicians to replace the men. Once the emergency medical technicians had examined her, she was transported to the hospital for treatment. For the next thirty-six hours, we were inseparable. She would not let anyone else near her, and she wanted me next to her—and holding her hand—any time someone entered the room.

Most of those thirty-six-hours were spent documenting her injuries onto an anatomically correct diagram, photographing each of the injuries, recording her statement, and filling out a written report. Part of being a police officer is separating emotions from the job. Law enforcement supports and serves the public; we do not show any emotions until afterward. There were so many emotions swirling around inside my mind, but my job was to be strong and accomplish the job efficiently and effectively. My controlling traits helped me accomplish my task.

While I was driving home, it hit like a ton of bricks without any warning. Before I knew what was happening, tears were rolling down my cheeks and my body was shaking from head to toe. My body felt like an iceberg as cold chills travel over me.

I pulled into a parking lot because I could no longer see to drive and cried until there were no tears left. I was emotionally drained and physically exhausted; I could not even drive the rest of the way home.

Charles knew what had occurred and came to pick me up. At home, he made me eat while I filled him in on what had been left out during our brief conversations—and then I slept for almost forty-eight hours. That was my last peaceful sleep for the next several weeks; upon Charles's insistence, I sought therapy. It took six weeks of therapy to deal with the turmoil from that atrocity. Within a few months of that incident, I resigned and turned in my badge. I could not handle it anymore. Charles encouraged me to return to college to finish my degree. Even with the therapy, that woman has never left my mind or heart. She often comes to mind. I still wonder if she is all right and what the outcome of the trial was. I guess I am seeking closure.

Returning to college should have been a reason to celebrate a dream coming true, but that was not the case. Life was out of control, and my downhill spiral into depression was in overdrive. On the way to my first day of classes, my hands were clammy, my heart was racing, and I was covered in a cold sweat. I called Charles to calm myself down. I thought it was a heart attack, and I headed for the emergency room. When my heart began to pound like a sledgehammer, Charles told me to pull over and call 911. They diagnosed panic attacks.

I said, "I do not have panic attacks!"

Even when the episode continued, I still denied that they were panic attacks. When I could not control something—or things did not go as I had planned—everything came to a stop. Our children were not allowed to cry or show weakness. If they did, they were told to put on their "big boy/girl panties" and get over it. They did not get their boo-boos kissed or get cuddled when they were hurt because I no longer knew how to feel those emotions. I had become numb to life and all the emotions that came with it. I was alive with a pulse and heartbeat, but I was not living.

The days turned into years, and life continued. However, some days, weeks, and months were unaccounted for. I had no memories and nothing to show for the time—just emptiness. I did not understand what was wrong. I did not know that the "thing" affecting our lives had a name. I knew there was something wrong, but I did not know how to fix it. Charles, the kids, and my career were all that kept me going during those years. If they had not been there, I would not be here today. On many days, they barely kept me living.

In 1999, a male helicopter pilot who resembled First Sergeant Higgans reached across to check my seatbelt harness. He brushed against my breast by accident, and even though he immediately apologized, it was too late. I broke into a cold sweat; time stood still, and I was back in that cold, dark storage room. The memories flashed by like an old black and white film that would never end.

I felt like that terrified eighteen-year-old girl from thirteen years ago; I just wanted to get out of there, away from him. I demanded to be taken back to the field office. I no longer cared about the mission. I wanted out of that helicopter and away from that pilot. My heart was pounding; I was getting dizzy and felt like throwing up. I tried breathing slowly and counting, but I had lost control. I felt like that scared young girl being raped again. As bad as that was, it was much worse by the end of the day. The meltdown escalated into a suicide attempt.

On the drive home, I called my mother and Charles to say my good-byes. Once home, I turned off my cell phone and ignored the ringing house phone. I sat down and began typing a good-bye letter to each of my kids.

Mom was terrified about me actually going through with it. She called Charles, and the two of them came up with a plan. Not knowing if I was going to kill myself at home or at the cemetery with Scott, they called law enforcement. Charles called the county sheriff's department, and Mom called the county sheriff for the cemetery. If they had not been worried enough to have the deputies check, it would have all ended that day.

I was lost in a stream of tears, trying to find the right words to say good-bye to my kids. I didn't hear the banging on the front door until it was kicked open and four officers rushed the house with guns drawn. I had been in their shoes several times as an officer, entering a scene without knowing what I was about to face.

Suddenly, there was nothing left in me. I just gave up on life and myself and collapsed into a heap in defeat. The deputies had to transport me to a mental hospital because I'd threatened suicide, had been a deputy, and owned guns. At the hospital, a mental evaluation was conducted, and it was determined that there was no immediate threat of suicide. Since there was no danger to others, they released me to Charles. He assured them that he would see to it I went to a therapist. I went for a while.

In fifteen years, Charles never knew the extent of the rapes or the damage they had caused. I did not allow him to see my weaknesses because I still felt ashamed and blamed myself. I wondered if I could have changed my accent; if I had spoken in a more refined manner, would he still have noticed me?

Over the last twenty-six years, I have blamed my "problem" on everything from Scott's dying, to being a single mother, to the kids, my husband, and even jobs. If you do not like yourself, how can you like anyone else? My emotional needs were satisfied through helping students, friends, and strangers—anyone except family. There was no emotional attachment to them; if it failed, it was okay. In all those years of hurt, anger, hopelessness, despair, and depression, it never occurred to me that the trauma of my rape—and the fact that I had compartmentalized it just as I had been expected to do—was the cause of my behavior. We did not mention the rape again; it was if it never happened—or that is what I needed to believe.

He Can Hurt Me Any Longer . . .

Blood boiled in my veins,

Like a flicker in every flame.

Tears fall from my eyes

Because my life is built on lies.

Controlled by fear,

I kept quiet for way too many years.

The secrets tucked away deep inside.

With a twisted mind,

He took his time.

I was lost in all the pain,

Wanting to wash it down the drain.

I wondered if it was my fault.

My fault for every rape and every assault.

Those dark memories still haunt my brain,

And still I feel I am the one to blame.

Every night I lie awake,

Wondering how much I can take.

If only someone would have listened

To my screams and pleas,

Maybe I could have ended it all,

Still be able to stand tall.

Enough is enough.

Tonight I will stay tough.

They will see that he can no longer hurt me.

To this day, depression, nightmares, low self-esteem, distrust, lack of affection, and emotional detachment still control my life at times. I now understand that those are symptoms of post-traumatic stress disorder. The conditions listed above are microscopic when you consider post-traumatic stress disorder in its entirety. No two people experience the same symptoms or even the same degree of symptoms. The same may be said about individual complaints; the symptoms you have today may not be the same symptoms that plague you during your next episode. It is hard for someone with mental health issues to ask for help, and the situation becomes even more complicated when dealing with soldiers. We were trained to be strong, independent, and to never show weakness, and that training carried over into civilian life. Just because soldiers take off their uniforms and move on in life does not mean that they leave all the training behind. That training is ingrained in us forever.

The doctors could find no reason why I had lost interest in family, friends, job, and life in general. They couldn't explain my depression, suicidal thoughts, or physical ailments. If they could not figure it out, how was I supposed to? Most doctors see so many patients in a day that they do not even have time—or take the time—to review medical records prior to a visit. How can they accurately treat patients when they are just a number?

After eight years, our family's primary doctor was shocked to hear that the VA had diagnosed me with post-traumatic stress disorder, borderline personality disorder, and major depression. She had treated me for insomnia, anxiety, and depression, but I never allowed her to see just how weak and in need of help I was. I always had to be strong—even if it killed me.

With a load of homework, I had planned to spend the day studying while the kids were at school. I lit a large fragrant candle on the end table and turned the stereo on to classical jazz. Charles was in Peru on business, and I had the house to myself. However, like most plans, it did not go as planned. Joseph missed the bus, which meant I had to drive him to school again. He hated walking down our long driveway to catch the bus. As many times as we showed him there was nothing to fear, it still terrified him. Austin Elementary was only five miles from the house. I rushed out the door to get him there on time, and I forgot all about the candle.

After dropping Joseph off, I decided to get a haircut before I went home. An hour later, I had to yield to a fire truck with its lights and horn going full force. As I continued to drive, I wondered where they were going. Did I want to follow them to see what was on fire or get home and do my homework while the house was quiet? That decision was made for me when they turned down our road. My curiosity became stronger as we got closer to my house. When we rounded the curve right before our driveway, reality sat in. They were going to our house!

The fire was burning so hot that we had to watch it burn for the first couple of hours. Our house had cedar planks and a tin roof; it was like lighting a match and dropping it in a gasoline can. Our ammo was exploding from the heat, which also kept them at bay. There were four fire departments, eight trucks, and numerous firefighters fighting our fire that day. As usual, the heat was hitting triple digits in Texas that August. With the heat from the fire, it was a dangerous job. The firefighters had to worry about the dangers of the actual fire and heat stroke.

Someone had called the school and told them about the house burning. As it tends to happen, things were blown out of proportion. Someone who had been on scene when the fire was first called in had noticed my car parked next to the porch. They assumed I was home, which would normally be true, but my car was low on gas and I drove

Charles's that morning. By the time it reached Corey, he had been told the house was engulfed—and no one had made it out of the house. He believed he had lost a parent for the second time. He expected me to be dead, and when he saw me, he ran and tackled me full force, crying and laughing at the same time.

Unfortunately, Nichole and Joseph had also heard the same thing. Even though Mrs. Crystal, a childhood friend's mother, told them it was not true, they did not believe it until they were able to see and hold me. Once the fire was out, nothing but the floor was standing. Our home resembled our lives; everything was in shambles.

Once the embers had cooled enough to allow the fire marshal to sift through the embers in order to determine the cause of the fire, a team of them looked for the culprit. They determined that a kitten had knocked over the candle and started the fire. Although our daughter knew her cat and kittens were not allowed in the house, she had been worried about the heat. She had been opening her window and shutting her door so they could come into her room during the day. Unfortunately, she had been in a rush and had not shut her door all the way.

Although three people shared the responsibility for the fire—Joseph for missing the bus, Nichole for letting her kittens in, and most of all, me for leaving a burning candle unattended—Charles blamed Nichole. I believe she is still troubled by it. She has never stopped blaming herself for something that was out of anyone's control. I wish I had said, "Shit happens. No one was killed, and everything else is replaceable."

When we should have all pulled together as a family, we dealt with it as if we were the only ones to lose something. In this instance, we failed the kids completely as parents. If only we could go back in time.

In addition to losing everything in the fire, the stress, the years of crazy controlling behavior, Charles's co-workers, and the kid's rebellions led to us decide to separate. He didn't really want to leave, but he was tired of walking on eggshells and watching the kids get criticized and put down all the time. His co-workers had convinced him that nothing any of us did was ever good enough for Charles. We never wanted to leave him, but we did during one of my meltdowns. To add insult to injury, not a single person from his office called or came to check on us. They sent a pilot who was from out of town and a mechanic. If my mother hadn't lived in the same town, we wouldn't have had anywhere to sleep that night.

All I ever wanted was for him to ask us to stay and to stand up for his family to his co-workers and friends. They often referred to me as "Bitch" amongst themselves, and they were always putting us down to Charles. Instead of speaking up for us, he let them tell him what to do. On one occasion when he was gone on a mission, they cleaned his desk of everything that had to do with us, placed it in a box, and put it in the storage room. Charles never took the items out and put them back on his desk, and he never confronted them about it. It just added more insult to injury. How could such a strong, moral, loyal man let his co-workers treat his family like this? Why did he allow this behavior? He once said his job was what paid our bills, but they should never have made him feel like he had to choose his job or us. However, that is exactly what they did.

During our separation, my car broke down on the freeway. I had to have AAA tow it to the closest dealership. They said it had mechanical issues that needed to be repaired before the car could be driven. Not having any other means of transportation, Charles was my only option. I gave in and called to see if he would let me use his truck since he drove his government car to and from work. He said he was heading out of the country on a mission, but he would leave the keys at his office.

The First Court of Appeals where I worked was in downtown Houston, and his office was in Conroe. I knew there was no way I would make it before his office closed for the day since the drive took at least an hour during rush hour. My other option was to call Corey, who was sixteen at the time, to ask him to pick up the keys for me. Since Corey did not drive, he had to ask a friend to take him to Charles's office. When the boys pulled up to the office building, they had the music up louder than it should have been.

Two of Charles's co-workers came out and started cussing and yelling at the boys, calling them thugs, punks, and dope heads. They searched the boys and the truck, but they didn't find anything. They refused to give Corey the keys and told him to get the fuck off the property and not to ever come back. I was beyond furious when Corey called and told me what had happened.

I called Charles's office to speak to the co-workers who had accosted the boys. When one answered, he began the conversation by calling me a bitch and told me how worthless my son was—and that he would end up in prison because he was just a dope headed punk. He said we had been nothing but trouble since Charles met us, and the smartest thing he had ever done was getting rid of us.

When I called Charles's boss, he called me a bitch and repeated what his co-worker had said. It sounded as if they had practiced a skit or something. Their words were the same. It was obvious that they had discussed what they would say when I called. The supervisor stated that the kids and I were banned from ever setting foot on the property again. If we did, the police would be called.

I tried to stay calm while I explained that I was at work and could not possibly get there before the office closed. He reluctantly agreed to let my daughter pick up the keys—as long as her brothers were not with her. Her little brother was only ten years old! Left with no other option, I had to call my thirteen-year-old daughter to ask her to see if her best friend's grandmother could take her to Charles's office. All of this because grown men—federal agents and a Harris County sheriff's deputy—felt the need to accost and intimidate children. Their behavior still mystifies me because I know their families were certainly not perfect. Why did they feel the need to crucify ours? Why did they feel entitled to make our family problems their own problems? What gave them the right to destroy a family just because they could?

When Charles returned from his assignment, his boss gave him an ultimatum: he had to choose his job with the Drug Enforcement Agency or his family. Loving him enough not to make him choose, and heartbroken knowing what his choice would be, we moved out. He did not even try to stop us; however, looking back at it, they really did not leave him with a choice.

He only had six years until he was eligible to retire; asking him to leave his job just was not an option for me at all. He had invested so much into his career, and flying was what he loved to do.

Blaming Charles and his co-workers would be a blatant lie. We were all at fault. Charles did not stand up to his co-workers, and his co-workers involved themselves personally in our relationship. The children, just being kids in general and through their defiance's, as neither Charles nor I were affectionate people and both being in law enforcement we saw no gray, it was black or white. I had control issues, mistrust, irrational behavior, and harsh judgments, especially with the ones who meant the most to me. If we had done things differently, our family would not be an emotional and mental mess. The kids and I still have explosive outbursts. They have the same attitude and emotional detachment, but it does not surprise me since that is what they grew up with.

After leaving Charles, we moved in with Mom in her little two-bedroom apartment. Two adults and three kids in such a small space did not work very well. The boys shared one room; mom and Nichole had the other one. I had the couch.

Charles and I came to an agreement for my portion of the insurance money from the fire. We had lost everything, but everyone was acting as if Charles was the only one who had suffered a loss. Using the money he gave us, I bought a house for us. I asked Mom to move in to help with the kids and the mortgage. It worked for a while, but living with a parent as an adult was more than I could handle. It caused problems between us, and Mom went to live with my sister and her family. I should have been more patient and understanding with my mom and the kids. However, by that point in life, I did not know how to be understanding or compassionate any longer.

Even though Charles and I were separated and lived apart, we continued to see each other and work on our relationship over the next three years. Each time I thought we were working it out, he would withdraw and disappear for weeks or months. Eventually, we spent more time apart than together. He would come around every weekend and then disappear for weeks with no calls. Eventually, we gave up on each other and moved on with our lives.

Everything changed in May 2006. I found a lump under my right armpit and made an appointment to see the doctor. She confirmed that it was definitely a lump, but she would need to refer me to a surgeon for a biopsy. When I asked what she thought it was, she explained that it was located in the lymph node. If it was lymphoid cancer, I had only a 20 percent survival rate.

Crying myself to sleep that night, all I could think about was my babies having to be raised without me. For Corey and Nichole, I was all they had left, and Joseph would have to be raised by an abusive alcoholic. When I thought of Charles, I decided that if I had a limited time to live, I did not want to spend another moment of it without him. The hurts and disappointments of the past just did not matter anymore. Our family was the only thing that mattered.

Charles was in Afghanistan, and I waited all night for him to sign onto Skype so we could talk. Just as I was about to give up, he signed on. I sent him an instant message and asked if we could talk. I was living with a boyfriend at the time, but Charles and the kids were all that mattered. He sent a message back that agreed. I told him about the lump and what the doctor had said about it possibly being cancer. I told him how very much I loved him—and how if my time was limited, I wanted to spend it with him. Over the next week, we talked nightly.

We moved back home in August 2006, and Charles and I renewed our relationship and commitment to each other. It took until October to get an appointment with a surgeon for the biopsy. I was terrified while the surgeon examined the lump. I felt like crying, but I tried to be strong at the same time. When he pressed on the lump, the pain made me grimace. He asked if it hurt when he pushed, and I said yes. He checked the other armpit and found that there was a huge painful lump there as well.

He excused himself and walked out of the exam room. He returned with a packet of papers. He started asking questions about foreign travel and contact with exotic animals. I hadn't. Looking perplexed, he asked me to fill the papers out.

I began reading the questions aloud and answering them. When I came to a question about being scratched by a cat in the last year, I automatically marked no. I have severe allergies to cats and dogs, but Nichole reminded me about a kitten I had allowed her to keep for a couple of weeks. She was gone all the time with her school activities, and the kitten hated me. It would hiss and claw me as if it was possessed any time I got near it. Therefore, she had to find it a new home.

When the surgeon came back in the room, I had just finished the questionnaire. As he flipped through the pages, he stopped on one and said, "The good news is you don't have lymphoid cancer. The bad news is that you have cat scratch fever, and there is no cure for it."

All that registered in my mind was the first part. It took a few minutes to realize what I had. As far as I knew, cat scratch fever was the name of a song.

He explained that cat scratch fever mimics lymphoid cancer, and that many primary doctors often misdiagnose it because they have never had a patient with it and are not familiar with it. There was no medication to treat it, and my body would have to build up its own antibodies. It could take a year or more for the symptoms to completely go away. He also explained that cat scratch fever never goes away; people just have to avoid cats for the rest of their lives. Getting scratched again it could start it all over, and it would take longer to recover.

After that scare, I was happier than I had been in a long time. All was right in my world, but it did not last. I just could not be happy—no matter how hard I tried or how bad I wanted to be. The nightmares had come back in full force; the doubt and suspicions from post-traumatic stress disorder were constant companions. I was angry and belittled Charles and the kids until the kids started rebelling and lashing out. One of the hardest things was never seeing the good in them. They were smart, loving kids who just wanted and needed their mom's love and approval, but all they received was criticism, unrealistic standards, and an emotionally unavailable mother. The vicious cycle kept going— no matter how hard I tried to stop it. Twenty-six years later, First Sergeant Higgans was still controlling me. Rape scars run deeper than time.

Regardless of how hard I tried to stay in control of my life and career, both of them were suffering. I started to spin out of control. I lost interest in my family, job, and students. I no longer loved teaching. I lost interest in life. I was a robot passing through time on this earth.

It all came to a head on September 1, 2009. On my way home from work, I was rear-ended by a man who was digging in his truck seat for a ringing cell phone. He was traveling at sixty-five miles an hour when he hit my truck. The truck bed was shoved six inches into the cab; the impact was so bad that it broke my neck, ruptured several discs in my back, and caused five hernias from the seatbelt. It required two surgeries to repair the damage to my neck.

My first surgery was in December 2009. They placed a metal plate in the front of my cervical spine in an attempt to stabilize the third and fourth discs where a bone graft had been placed. The bone graft did not take, requiring a second surgery. The second surgery was in May 2010. Metal rods were inserted on each side of my cervical spine to stabilize the third, fourth and fifth discs. The surgery was successful, and I was excited to return to teaching my high school criminal justice students.

Unfortunately, due to absences, I was reprimanded for the frequently requested leave. The principal explained that it was not fair to the students to have so many substitute teachers, and the cost was hurting the district's operating budget. Knowing that more surgeries would be required along with recuperation, physical therapy, and pain management, I resigned from teaching. I loved my students and loved teaching them. It broke my heart when he said they were suffering because of me. Resigning devastated me, but I knew it was what the kids deserved. That wreck took my health, job, and independence away. The multiple surgeries, recovery time, and self-pity enabled depression to sink its claws into me again.

I had to have four abdominal surgeries to repair the hernias. Due to being immobile, I began to gain weight, which led to me becoming even more depressed. With each surgery, I became even more discouraged about ever recovering. The vicious circle felt endless. When I recovered from one surgery and felt hopeful again, I would be told that another surgery was needed—and it would begin all over.

The weight seemed to just pile on, which catapulted me to an even deeper depression and despair. I lost touch with family, friends, and former students. I stopped caring about life and everything in general. Bed became a safe haven and a prison. I only got out of bed to eat or use the restroom. When I was asked to do something, I would make excuses. The days turned into weeks, the weeks turned into months, and the months turned into years. Three years of my life was wasted in a world of dark despair and hopelessness.

In June 2012, during a visit to the Veterans Outpatient Clinic, I picked up a card for the Veterans Crisis Line. That evening when getting back home, I cleaned out my wallet. I put the card on the nightstand with some receipts to be burnt. I completely forgot about it until I was seconds away from committing suicide. Had it not been for that card, I would not be here to tell my story.

In July 2012, I finally mustered the courage to report my rapes to the army's Criminal Investigation Division. I was blessed to be assigned to Special Agent Keyes. Not dealing very well with men, I was extremely leery when he called and asked to come out to take my statement. He explained that there would be two army special agents assigned to the case, and he would be the lead investigator. He and his partner would be the ones to investigate the case.

When they arrived, they were both polite and sensitive because of their awareness that a victim's trauma can be relived while telling of it. They gave the option of meeting somewhere else or in my home. My home was my safety zone, which made me feel safe enough to talk.

Special Agents Keyes should train all military sexual assault investigators. He was compassionate, reassuring, and tenacious. Although my case was twenty-six years old, he investigated and worked my case as if it had occurred yesterday. In the last twelve months, he has kept me updated every step of the way and has returned my calls even when there is nothing new to tell me. He has encouraged me to tell my story and take my life back.

With a heavy heart, he informed me that my case was being closed with the finding that the rapes occurred as reported and that First Sergeant Higgans—who was retired and collecting a military pension check—would be registered in the database as a felony sex offender.

Any time his information was checked or run by law enforcement—for credit, employment, or any number of things—it would show him as a felony sex offender.

Special Agent Keyes explained that the VA could take his medical benefits away, but because of the age of the case, they would not bring him back to active duty to prosecute him. It was not the closure I was hoping for, but the necessary closure has been found in writing this book. If it has helped even one person, then the pain has been worth it.

In September 2012, depression took a hold of me and would not let go. I was only seconds away from committing suicide when I looked down and saw the card on the nightstand. I do not remember dialing the crisis hotline, but if the operator had not answered so quickly, I would not be here today. She listened and talked with me until I was in a rational frame of mind. Once she was positive that I was past my critical stage, she referred me to my local veteran's clinic. She made an appointment for thirty minutes later. That card and the crisis operator who answered my call saved my life.

My story continues, but I have two heartbreaking stories of two very special women who died as a result of military sexual trauma.

The first story is about Carri Leigh Goodwin, United States Marine Corps.

Carri Leigh Goodwin, USMC

In August of 2007, at the age of eighteen, Carri Leigh Goodwin of Ohio enlisted in the United States Marine Corps to make her father, Gary Noling, a former marine proud. During her time in the Marine Corps, Carri reported a rape. Instead of supporting Carri and having her allegations taken seriously, she felt that the Marine Corps did not do enough to help her. Similar to what many survivors reported, the blame for the rape was placed on the survivor instead of the perpetrator. Carri was bullied by her commander for reporting a rape and was eventually forced out of the Marine Corps for personality disorder, the military's scapegoat diagnoses to discharge rape victims.

According to an external investigation, the alleged rapist had been accused of another rape in 2006 at Camp Pendleton but was able to continue serving. The alleged rapist did receive a non-judicial punishment (NJP) for the rape of Carri Goodwin, but that was all. He is still in the Marine Corps. A non-judicial punishment in the United States Armed Forces is a form of military justice authorized by Article 15 of the Uniform Code of Military Justice. Non-judicial punishment permits commanders to administratively discipline troops without a court-martial. Punishment can range from reprimand to reduction in rank, correctional custody, confinement on bread and water/diminished rations (aboard ships only), loss of pay, extra duty, and/or restrictions. The receipt of non-judicial punishment does not constitute a criminal conviction (it's equivalent to a civil action), but it is often placed in the service record of the individual.

The day Carri was discharged from service, her father, sister, and brother picked her up from the bus station, happy that she was back home safely. Five days later, at the age of twenty, Carri drank herself to death. To make matters worse, her sister was eventually charged with involuntary manslaughter and furnishing alcohol to an underage person. Because of the effects of military sexual trauma, an entire family has been turned upside down, losing a daughter due to the military's lack of resources to help a survivor in need.

According to a journal that Carri left behind, she confessed that the pain of the rape and the response from the Marine Corps were unbearable. Carri had an alcohol blood content of .46, which was six times the legal limit. Medication given to her by the Marine Corps, including Zoloft, stopped the alcohol from going through her liver, and it went straight to her blood. She had signed up with wishes to be deployed to a war zone, to go to combat, and defend her country. Instead, Carri was raped, blamed for the rape, and betrayed at the hands of her command.

Carri left behind three journals. Below is a picture of one of the drawings found in her journal.

A picture she left behind showed how the rape affected her.

Staff Sergeant Sophie Champoux

Sophie Christine Lisa Champoux, twenty-five, of Fort Stewart, Georgia, died on September 30, 2011. She was born on July 5, 1986, in Orlando to Denis Jean Joseph Champoux and Suzette Perkins Champoux. She was the oldest of three children. She was a former Clermont resident and member of Clermont Bible Church until she relocated to New Jersey in 2006. She was a sergeant in the US Army, stationed at Fort Stewart.

She was survived by her mother, Suzette Champoux of Clermont; father Denis Champoux, Centennial, Colorado; brothers Ian Champoux, Orlando, and Noah Champoux, Winter Park, and paternal grandparents Paul and Celine Champoux, Dover, Florida.

The account of Sophie Champoux's rape and death were told by Sophie's mother.

No parent should lose his or her child like this. Sophie was an honest young woman who had a great relationship with her family. Sophie played softball, practiced Taekwondo, and played both the guitar and drums. She participated in Junior Reserve Officer Training

Corps in high school and earned a degree in graphic arts from a local technical college.

She had always wanted to be a soldier and scored in the 98th percentile on her Armed Service Vocational Aptitude Battery (ASVAB). She was well on her way to success when she decided to join the United States Army.

Despite a successful career and deployments, fellow soldiers raped Sophie on three separate occasions. She died in September 2011. The Department of Defense told her family that she committed suicide; not believing them, her family demanded an investigation.

Sophie excelled at boot camp as a soldier, and at graduation, everything seemed fine to her family. She went to technical school at Fort Sam Houston and became an army medic. She seemed excited to be at Fort Sam Houston and began to think about becoming a physician assistant or a doctor.

In three and a half years, Sophie was raped while she was on stationed in White Sands, New Mexico, while serving in Sharan, Afghanistan, and while stationed at Fort Stewart in Georgia. The same man who raped her in Afghanistan stalked and raped her again at Fort Stewart.

Her rapist at Fort Stewart confessed to Criminal Investigative Division (CID), and then he retracted his statements. He stole an army vehicle and was arrested for DUI. The rapist was sentenced to a meager forty months in military prison for her rape, stealing an army vehicle, going AWOL, and DUI.

Sophie called her mother from Afghanistan and said, "Mom, send me Ka-Bar, a large military knife, because I cannot go to the bathroom safely. I have more to fear from my own fellow soldiers than from any Afghani enemy." Sophie was never scared of the Afghani citizens; however, she was terrified of her fellow soldiers.

While stationed at Fort Stewart, Sophie was found with a gunshot wound behind her right ear. Her time of death was 10:30 p.m. on Friday, September 30, 2011. Her mother was not informed of her death until 1:00 a.m. on October 2, 2012.

Army investigators told Sophie Champoux's mother that Sophie committed suicide for the insurance money and ruled her death a suicide. Sophie's family did not believe it was suicide then or today!

*   *   *

As promised my story continues.

Due to my being raped during AIT, I spent many years disassociating myself from the army. I never felt like I belonged or deserved to be at the veteran's hospital or outpatient clinics. I did not feel as if I deserved the medical treatment and always felt out of place. I stopped going to them for treatment of any kind. When I was taken right in to see the psychologist, I was so thankful that I did not have to sit in the lobby like a fat calf on the auction block. Sitting there with all those men staring at me always made my skin crawl. I just wanted to disappear.

Dr. Richter was kind, compassionate, and gentle while asking me what had led me to call the crisis hotline. He spent a several hours listening to me talk, and I finally told him what had happened to me all those long years ago while in the army and about the craziness and depression that had been consuming me. He diagnosed post-traumatic stress disorder. He was the first person to explain that what I had been experiencing had a name. My post-traumatic stress disorder was a direct result of military sexual trauma (MST).

Sexual assault and harassment damages a survivor's self-esteem and trust. Some survivors are criticized or judged by others who do not understand what it is like to be violated. These side effects can lead to even more suffering while the person tries to recover. Common aftereffects for survivors of sexual assault and harassment include post-traumatic stress disorder, depression, feeling on guard, suicidal thoughts, anger, anxiety, shame, self-blame, strong, painful emotions, difficulties in relationships, emotional numbness, difficulties at work, problems with alcohol and drugs, sexual problems, sleep problems, physical health problems, attention and memory problems, and spiritual crises.

Sexual assault and harassment are like a continuum of behaviors, with assault and rape at the extreme end of that continuum, they are often interconnected, beginning with harassment and leading to assault or starting with assault and then the harassment begins. Victims may have similar responses to them. While sexual assault and harassment may have a profound impact, people can heal. Those who seek support tend to recover faster and more completely after stress or trauma. Tell someone you trust what has happened—do not struggle alone.

MST, sexual assault, and sexual harassment are traumatic events. Like other kinds of trauma, sexual assault and/or harassment can often negatively affect the survivors for years after the event. Victims often feel afraid, helpless, horrified, humiliated, and confused. If the trauma is upsetting enough, some victims go completely numb and cut themselves off from the experience.

Other survivors say their feelings about the experience were absent for a long time and then reappeared. Many people who have experienced a traumatic event will eventually display symptoms of post-traumatic stress disorder. They are often plagued with guilt, worry, depression, anger issues that more often than not lead to troubled relationships with spouses, children, family, friends, and co-workers. In addition, they are susceptible to panic attacks, which can cause agitation, excitability, dizziness, and lightheadedness, fainting, racing or pounding hearts, headaches, and an increase in mental and physical health issues.

While male sexual assault and harassment are vastly underreported in the military, one-estimate claims 3.5 percent of male service members are sexually assaulted while in the military, and 1.2 percent are raped. A 2006 report found 1.8 percent of active duty men were sexually assaulted in a single year. Statistics of sexual harassment vary, ranging from 6-38 percent of men in the military.

Female veterans who have been sexually assaulted in the military are nine times more likely to develop post-traumatic stress disorder than military women who are not. On a broader scale, military sexual assault affects more than just the individual victims. It also negatively affects mission readiness and destroys the trust needed among service members responsible for protecting each other. Preservation of military readiness is vitally important; however, it is a casualty of military sexual trauma as well.

I bet you are asking what exactly post-traumatic stress disorder is. I asked myself that question when my psychologist suggested that I might have it. Post-traumatic stress disorder is a debilitating anxiety disorder that occurs after experiencing or witnessing a traumatic event that involves either a real or a perceived threat of injury or death. This can include a natural disaster, combat, assault, physical or sexual abuse, or other trauma. Post-traumatic stress disorder sufferers have a heightened sense of danger and impending doom. Their natural fight-or-flight response is damaged, causing them to feel stressed or fearful at all times, even in safe situations. Most people who experience a traumatizing event will not develop post-traumatic stress disorder. However, because women are more likely to experience more high-impact trauma, they are more likely to develop post-traumatic stress disorder than men. Children are less likely to experience post-traumatic stress disorder after trauma than adults, especially if they are less than ten years of age.

How do you know if you or a loved one has post-traumatic stress disorder? The symptoms of post-traumatic stress disorder can disrupt normal activities and interfere with a person's ability to function. Words, sounds, or situations can act as reminders of trauma.

Symptoms fall into three groups:

1. Reliving the trauma, which consists of flashbacks, in which it feels as if the event is occurring again, intrusive, vivid memories of the event, frequent nightmares of the event, and mental or physical discomfort when reminded of the event

2. Avoidance, which includes emotional apathy, detachment from or lack of interest in daily activities, amnesia (memory loss) about the actual event or parts of the actual event, the inability to express feelings, and avoidance of people or situations that are reminders of the event.

3. Increased arousal, which is characterized by difficulty concentrating, startling easily, exaggerated response to startling events, constantly feeling on guard (hypervigilance), irritability, bouts of anger, and difficulty falling or staying asleep.

My psychologist told me about a post-traumatic stress disorder/ military sexual trauma program at Houston's Michael E. DeBakey VA Medical Center. The Women's Inpatient Specialty Environment of Recovery (WISER) is a trauma-informed, intensive treatment approach tailored specifically for female veterans with a diagnosis of post-traumatic stress disorder, mood or anxiety disorder, and co-occurring substance abuse/dependence.

WISER programming is grounded in the highest level of trauma-focused, evidence-based treatments, which are provided mostly in group therapy. The twenty-five-day program is housed in an inpatient, psychiatric setting. After completing the program and acquiring new skills, techniques, and insights to improve quality of life, the veteran will return to her home clinic and resume outpatient treatment. WISER values are based on recovery, safety and trust, effective coping skills, empowerment, healthy intimate relationships, quality of life, mindfulness, connection to others, and wisdom of women. The types of therapies are dialectical behavior skills, cognitive processing therapy, seeking safety, women's wellness and nutrition classes, interpersonal process groups, cognitive behavioral therapy, skills groups, occupational/recreational therapy, and individual therapy (when appropriate).

I was scheduled to enter the program the following week. The idea of being admitted did not rank very high with me, but I also knew that if I did not go, I probably would not survive. It was an intensive program, and I wanted to leave on a couple of different occasions, but the staff was effective in keeping you there and keeping you on track.

I was one of nine women in the program. We ranged from the Women's Army Corps (WAC) era to Operation Enduring Freedom (OIF). It was quite an emotional rollercoaster during those three and a half weeks. We started by talking about ourselves, why we were in the program, and what we hoped to get out of it. We moved into our post-traumatic stress disorder traumas through Cognitive Processing Therapy (CPT). CPT conceptualizes post-traumatic stress disorder as a disorder of "non-recovery" in which erroneous beliefs about the causes and consequences of traumatic event produce strong negative emotions and prevent accurate processing of the trauma memory and natural emotions emanating from the event.

Although post-traumatic stress disorder is currently classified as an anxiety disorder, most people with post-traumatic stress disorder experience a range of emotions, including horror, anger, shame, guilt, sadness, and fear. A significant contributor to the interruption of the natural recovery process is the ongoing use of avoidance as a coping method. By avoiding the trauma memory and situations that trigger reactions, people with post-traumatic stress disorder limit opportunities to process the traumatic experience and gain a more adaptive understanding.

CPT incorporates trauma-specific cognitive techniques to help individuals with post-traumatic stress disorder more accurately appraise these "stuck points" and progress toward recovery. The primary focus of CPT is to help patients gain an understanding of—and modify the meaning attributed to—the traumatic event. In pursuit of this objective, an important goal of CPT is decreasing the pattern of avoiding the trauma memory in order for beliefs and meanings to be assessed and understood in their original context.

The initial phase of treatment consists of education regarding post-traumatic stress disorder, thoughts, and emotions. The therapist develops rapport with patients by establishing a common understanding of the problems experienced by the patients and outlining the cognitive theory of PTSD development and maintenance. This information is essential for helping patients understand the rationale and goals of therapy.

Patients are asked to write an impact statement to identify how they understand why the events occurred and the impacts that they had on their beliefs about themselves, others, and the world. In this phase of treatment, a large focus is on the identification of automatic thoughts and increasing awareness of the relationship between a person's thoughts and feelings. Specifically, patients are taught to identify stuck points, which are problematic beliefs that interfere with recovery from traumatic experiences. *It is my fault. I should have known that he would attack me. I should have fought harder.*

The next phase of post-traumatic stress disorder involves formal processing of the trauma. Patients are asked to write a detailed account of the most traumatic experience, which they read to the therapist in session. By writing this account, patients break the pattern of avoidance and increase the process of dissipating the strong emotions that have yet to "run the natural course of recovery."

Emotional processing continues throughout the course of post-traumatic stress disorder as patients discuss their traumatic experiences to clarify and modify maladaptive beliefs. Clinicians use Socratic dialog to discuss the details of the trauma, which helps patients gently challenge their thinking about their traumatic event and become increasingly able to consider the context in which the event occurred. This goal is decreasing self-blame and guilt and increasing acceptance. The Socratic Method is based on the understanding that patients need to engage in their own process of knowing. By asking questions, rather than providing interpretations or advice, patients are able to unfold their own insights.

An alternative model of post-traumatic stress disorder that has been found to be equally effective, and perhaps more efficient, is to conduct the standard protocol without the written accounts. This method relies instead on Socratic dialogue between therapist and client to bring out the details of the trauma that might refute the client's assumptions and self-assessment about their worst traumatic experience.

The final phase of treatment focuses on teaching patients the cognitive skills necessary to identify, evaluate, and modify their beliefs as necessary regarding all traumatic events they have experienced. Patients focus on the stuck points and work to better understand and challenge habitual and unrealistic conclusions about their traumatic experiences (e.g., "This means that no one can be trusted in any way"). The skills learned in this phase of treatment are helpful to empower patients to "become their own therapists" and to learn how to engage in adaptive coping post-treatment.

The final phase of treatment focuses on five themes that have been identified as areas in which beliefs are commonly impacted by a traumatic experience. These themes include safety, trust, power/control, esteem, and intimacy. Patients learn to recognize how their beliefs may have become over-generalized based on their traumatic experiences and how their current functioning and quality of life have been impacted as a result. They utilize these new cognitive skills to re-evaluate these beliefs and develop alternate ways of viewing the world that are ultimately more balanced and adaptive.

Another type of therapy used for post-traumatic stress disorder patients is exposure therapy. In exposure therapy, the goal is to have less fear about certain memories. It is based on the idea that people learn to fear thoughts, feelings, and situations that remind them of a past traumatic event. By repeatedly talking about trauma with a therapist, people learn to get control of thoughts and feelings about the trauma. They learn not to be afraid of those memories.

This may be hard at first. It might seem strange to think about stressful things on purpose. However, people will feel less overwhelmed over time. With the help of a therapist, people can change how they react to stressful memories. Talking in a secure place makes this easier.

People focus on memories that are less upsetting before talking about worse ones. This "desensitization allows them to deal with bad memories a little bit at a time. The therapist may ask a patient to remember many bad memories at once. This "flooding" helps people learn to not feel overwhelmed. They may practice different ways to relax during stressful memories. Breathing exercises are sometimes used for this.

Eye Movement Desensitization and Reprocessing (EMDR) is another type of therapy for post-traumatic stress disorder. Like other kinds of counseling, it can help change how people react to memories of trauma. While thinking of or talking about memories, they focus on other stimuli (eye movements, hand taps, and other sounds). The therapist may move a hand near your face, and you will follow this movement with your eyes. Experts are still learning how EMDR works. Studies have shown that it may help people have fewer post-traumatic stress disorder symptoms.

Other kinds of counseling may be helpful for recovery. Group therapy is one of them. Many people want to talk about trauma with others who have had similar experiences. Group therapy includes talking with a group of people who also have been through a trauma and have post-traumatic stress disorder.

Sharing your story with others may help you feel more comfortable talking about your trauma. This can help you cope with your symptoms, memories, and other parts of your life. Group therapy helps you build relationships with others who understand what you have endured. You learn to deal with emotions, such as shame, guilt, anger, rage, and fear. Sharing with the group also can help build self-confidence and trust. You will learn to focus on your present life instead of feeling overwhelmed by the past.

Brief psychodynamic psychotherapy is another type of therapy. In this type of therapy, you learn ways of dealing with emotional conflicts caused by trauma. This therapy helps you understand how the past affects the way you feel now. Your therapist can help you identify what triggers stressful memories and other symptoms, find ways to cope with intense feelings about the past, and become more aware of your thoughts and feelings so you can change your reactions to them and raise your self-esteem.

Family therapy can also be used in post-traumatic stress disorder treatment. Post-traumatic stress disorder can—and more often than not—affect the entire family. Children and partners may not understand why you get angry sometimes or why you are under so much stress. They may feel scared, guilty, or angry about your condition. Family therapy is a type of counseling that involves the whole family. A therapist helps the entire family communicate, maintain good relationships, and cope with tough emotions.

In family therapy, each person can express his or her fears and concerns. It is important to be honest about your feelings and to listen to others. You can talk about your post-traumatic stress disorder symptoms and triggers. You also can discuss the important parts of your treatment and recovery. By doing this, your family will be better prepared to help you. You may consider having individual therapy for your post-traumatic stress disorder symptoms and family therapy to help with your relationships.

Medications may also play an important role in treating post-traumatic stress disorder. Some of the most common medications prescribed are antidepressants, anti-anxiety drugs, and sleep aids to decrease the frequency of intrusive, frightening thoughts and allow you to get some rest.

Many people who suffer from post-traumatic stress disorder turn to illicit drugs and alcohol to cope with their symptoms. While these methods may temporarily alleviate symptoms of post-traumatic stress disorder, they do not treat the underlying cause of stress and can make some symptoms worse. If you have developed a problem with substance abuse, a therapist may also recommend a twelve-step program to reduce any dependency on drugs or alcohol.

What is the outlook for people with post-traumatic stress disorder? Early treatment can help alleviate symptoms and provide effective strategies for coping with intrusive thoughts, memories, and flashbacks. Cognitive Behavioral Therapy (CBT) treatment for post-traumatic stress disorder often lasts for three to six months. Other types of treatment for post-traumatic stress disorder can last longer. If you have additional mental health problems, treatment may last for two years or longer.

The most important aspect of post-traumatic stress disorder treatment is the patient. You have to be a willing participant in your treatment plan. You should be aware that no treatment will "wipe the slate clean" and erase all memories of the event. You have to implement the skills you are taught and apply them to your daily living. If you experience a trigger or a setback, it is expected, but you need to use your skills to work your way through it with the help of your therapist.

It has been nine months since I graduated from the WISER program. I am not free of my post-traumatic stress disorder symptoms, but I experience them less often. I no longer barricade myself in my bedroom when my husband is on his rotations in Afghanistan, and I no longer sleep with my Smith and Wesson locked and loaded on his pillow. I am currently working on getting out of the house to go shopping or just have my nails done. I make most of my medical and mental health appointments opposed to canceling or no-showing 90 percent of the time. Most importantly, I do not rely on my children to do everything for me.

My relationship with my husband has improved so much because I do not live every day waiting for the worst to happen and trying to sabotage our relationship. I had to be in control; if I was going to be hurt, I was going to be the cause of that pain—and not anyone else. I still have nightmares when it is storming, and I still jump when someone approaches me from behind and startles me, but I no longer have major meltdowns. I have found that many of the skills taught in the WISER program still serve me today.

There are many programs available for veterans.

Women's Inpatient Specialty Environment of Recovery (WISER)

http://www.houston.va.gov/services/women/WISER.asp

Women's Inpatient Specialty Environment of Recovery is a trauma-informed, intensive treatment approach tailored specifically for women veterans with a diagnosis of one. Women's Inpatient Specialty Environment of Recovery Women's Inpatient Specialty Environment of Recovery, mood or anxiety disorder, and co-occurring substance abuse/dependence. Women's Inpatient Specialty Environment of

Recovery programming is grounded in the highest level of trauma-focused evidence-based treatments, which are provided mostly in group therapy. WISER is a twenty-five-day program housed in an inpatient, psychiatric setting at the Michael E. DeBakey VA Medical Center in Houston. After completing the program and acquiring new skills, techniques, and insights to improve her quality of life, the veteran will return to her home clinic and resume outpatient treatment.

There are some wonderful support/advocacy groups for military sexual trauma survivors. I was blessed this year to be accepted by Expedition Balance to participate in a three-day veteran's retreat. We were taught yoga and meditation and participated in outdoor recreation activities, such as canoeing, horseback riding, zip-lining, and bicycling. The activities were designed to help veterans in need of moral and physical support to feel good about themselves again.

Expedition Balance

http://www.expeditionbalance.org/

Expedition Balance supports the recovery of US combat veterans by offering a balanced approach to wellness through group outdoor recreation, spiritual awareness, creative expression, physical fitness, and healthy lifestyle education.

F7 Group

http://www.f7group.com/

F7 Group is the premier resource for female veterans and women in military families and is dedicated to securing and providing resources, training, mentoring, and support.

F7 Group recognizes and believes in the courage, value, and abilities of the women who serve our country in many different capacities. Some serve in uniform, and some are the support system for our military personnel.

They provide the fundamental tools, systems, and networks through retreats, boot camps, and technology-based platforms. They provide these services though sponsorships and donations made to the organization. In addition, they provide corporate trainings through our VETPro program, teaching companies "how to speak vet."

Some of the services F7 Group offers include:

- weekend retreats
- three-day intensive entrepreneurial boot camps with leading industry experts
- half-day skills training, mentoring programs, and workshops
- VETPro, a corporate training program designed to teach companies how to attract, retain, and accommodate
- grants for WIMSA Memorial
- scholarships for F7 affiliate programs, Copperrock Business Solutions, and many others
- For more information, contact president and co-founder Victoria A. Wegwert at (956) 346-4255

Service Women Action Network

http://servicewomen.org/

SWAN's mission is to transform military culture by securing equal opportunity and freedom to serve without discrimination, harassment, or assault; and to reform veterans' services to ensure high quality healthcare and benefits for women veterans and their families. They accomplish their mission through policy reform, media advocacy, litigation, and direct services.

Protect Our Defenders

http://www.protectourdefenders.com/

Protect Our Defenders is a human rights organization that honors, supports, and gives voices to the brave women and men in uniform who have been raped or sexually assaulted by fellow service members. They seek to fix the military training, investigation, and adjudication systems related to sexual violence and harassment—systems that often re-victimize assault survivors by blaming them while failing to prosecute perpetrators.

A Black Rose

http://www.ablackrose.org/mst-information.html

The organization's main goal is to show the nation that they will no longer stand for men and women in the armed forces being abused and sexually assaulted. They do this through the Black Rose Campaign.

Nothing is more painful than holding the trauma of abuse inside. A Black Rose aims to create a safe—and if need be—anonymous way to speak out on the topic of abuse in the military. This issue is real, and support proves that.

Military brothers and sisters serving this country still face startling statistical atrocities. The organization works toward preventing abuse and harassment. They believe that all members of the armed forces deserve to serve without fear of being abused by fellow soldiers.

Department of Veterans Affairs Response to Military Sexual Trauma by Amy Street, PhD

National Military Sexual Trauma Support Team Department of Veterans Affairs http://www.ablackrose.org/uploads/4/5/0/3/4503108/street_dcoe_ presentation.pdf

Women Veterans Foundation

http://www.womenveteransfoundation.org/

The organization is demanding immediate protection from perpetrators. They demand accountability and punishment to all who foster an environment of bias and retaliation. This would begin to restore the trust in our service members to report. The people demand "reporting and control to prosecute" sexual assaults be taken outside the "chain of command" to protect all service members. We must have "real" immediate reforms with the Congressional Brandon H.R.1593 STOPAct and/or Senate Bill 967 Military Justice Improvement Act And this will be accomplished by removing "reporting and control to prosecute" sexual assaults outside the "chain of command".

The organization is committed to promoting healing and providing advocates and resources for veterans and their families affected by MST, military sex post-traumatic stress disorder, post-traumatic stress disorder, and homelessness. Soldiers who have been sexually harassed, assaulted, and/or raped in the military are not alone. For support, please visit "MST Advocates." We are veterans helping veterans. A "Band of Brothers and Sisters" uniquely qualified to support and helps each other.

*   *   *

There is no cure for post-traumatic stress disorder, but it is manageable with the right treatment program. I have found that yoga and meditation have helped my mental and physical health. I enjoy making hand-constructed jewelry and writing poetry. They are both relaxing and rewarding when I am stressed. They key is to find what works for you and work it!

It does not matter if you just returned from a deployment or have been home for forty years. If you experienced military sexual trauma, sexual assault, or any other traumatic life event, it is never too late to get professional treatment or support for post-traumatic stress disorder. Starting counseling or treatment as soon as possible can keep your symptoms from getting worse.

Stormie Dunn

Post-Traumatic Stress Disorder (PTSD) Care for Everyone

Find a therapist. Get information, phone numbers, and websites to help locate care for post-traumatic stress disorder. Seek help for family and friends since it affects them as well.

Learn about resources to help them deal with taking care of someone with post-traumatic stress disorder.

Post-Traumatic Stress Disorder Care for Veterans, Military, and Families

Go to http://www.ptsd.va.gov/public/pages/help-for-veterans-with-ptsd.asp to learn how to enroll for Veterans Administration's health care and get an assessment. All Veterans Administration's medical centers provide post-traumatic stress disorder care, as do many clinics.

Some Veterans Administrations have programs specializing in post-traumatic stress disorder treatment. Use the Veterans Administration post-traumatic stress disorder program locator to find a program. http://www.va.gov/directory/guide/ptsd_flsh.asp

Post-Traumatic Stress Disorder Coach Online http://1.usa. gov/18sp7OI

There are tools to aid in managing stress. "Post-Traumatic Stress Disorder Coach Online" is for anyone who needs help with upsetting feelings. Trauma survivors, their families, or anyone coping with stress can benefit. Problems addressed are worry or anxiety, anger, sadness, hopelessness, sleep problems, trauma reminders, avoidance of stressful situations, disconnection from people, disconnection from reality, and problem-solving skills.

If you are a war veteran, find a vet center to help with the transition from military to civilian life (http://www.vetcenter.va.gov/).

Call the 24/7 Veteran Combat Call Center 1-877-WAR-VETS (1-877-927-8387) to talk to another combat veteran.

The DoD's Defense Centers of Excellence (DCoE) 24/7 Outreach Center for Psychological Health and Traumatic Brain Injury provides information and helps locate resources. Call 1-866-966-1020 or e-mail resources@dcoeoutreach.org.

Military OneSource

Call 24/7 for counseling and resources 1-800-342-9647. Get Help with VA PTSD care, benefits, or claims (http://www.ptsd.va.gov/public/get_help_with_va.asp).

The information in this book is for educational purposes only. It is not a substitute for informed medical advice or training. Do not use this information to diagnose or treat a mental health problem without consulting a qualified health or mental health care provider.

1. *The Daily Beast, NewsWeek Magazine*, "The Military's Secret Shame,"

   http://www.thedailybeast.com/newsweek/2011/04/03/the-military-s-secret-shame.html

   Ellison, Jesse, Apr 3, 2011, 1:00 a.m.

2. Sexual Violence Victims Say Military Justice System Is "Broken"

   http://www.npr.org/2013/03/21/174840895/sexual-violence-victims-say-military-justice-system-is-broken

Lawrence, Quil and Penaloza, Marisa, March 21, 2013 3:05
a.m.

3. Women Escape War Only to Suffer Sexual Trauma and Be
    Denied Proper Help

    http://www.care2.com/causes/women-escape-war-only-
    to-suffer-sexual-trauma-and-be-denied-proper-help.
    html#ixzz2ecQaaTSV

    Josephs, Kevin, September 10, 2013, 2:30 p.m.

4. *Army Times*, 18 Veterans Commit Suicide Each Day

    http://www.armytimes.com/article/20100422/
    NEWS/4220330/18-veterans—commit-suicide-each-day

    Maze, Rick, Apr. 22, 2010, 02:56 p.m.

5. American Psychiatric Association (2013). *Diagnostic and
    Statistical Manual of Mental Disorders* (Fifth ed.). Arlington,
    VA: American Psychiatric Publishing, 271-280.

6. National Collaborating Centre for Mental Health (UK) (2005).
    "Post-Traumatic Stress Disorder: The Management of PTSD
    in Adults and Children in Primary and Secondary Care."

NICE Clinical Guidelines, No. 26. Gaskell (Royal College of Psychiatrists).

Retrieved 1 June 2013.

7. "Military Sexual Trauma," US Department of Veteran Affairs.

http://www.mentalhealth.va.gov/msthome.asp

Retrieved March 12, 2013.

8. NCPTSD Fact Sheet: Military Sexual Trauma: Issues in Caring for Veterans

http://www.ncptsd.va.gov/ncmain/ncdocs/fact_shts/military_sexualtrauma.html?opm=1&rr=rr145&srt=d&echorr=true

Hillard, G. (2007)

9. Scars of War Run Deep for Many Female Vets. All Things Considered; National Public Radio (transcript)

http://www.npr.org/templates/story/story.php?storyId=15005484

Accessed February 26, 2009, Goldman, Russell. (2007)

10. Pentagon Reports Increase in Sex Assaults as VA Opens New

   Facility for Women, ABC News Online

   http://www.afterdeployment.org/sites/default/files/pdfs/client-

   handouts/mst-sexual-assault-harassment.pdf

About the Author

Stormie Dunn is a US Army veteran and survivor of Military Sexual Trauma. Through her recovery she has become an advocate for fellow MST victims and their families. She graduated from Sam Houston State University with a degree in criminal justice; is a resident of Fairfield Bay, Arkansas, with her husband of sixteen years and is the mother of three children, a stepson, and the grandmother of three beautiful grandchildren. She is active in her church and community and continues her road to recovery at the Little Rock Veterans Administration Hospital.